Never Stop Driving

A BETTER LIFE BEHIND THE WHEEL

Never Stop Driving

A BETTER LIFE BEHIND THE WHEEL

BY LARRY WEBSTER, ZACH BOWMAN,
JACK BARUTH, AND BRETT BERK

motorbooks

Brimming with creative inspiration, how-to projects, and useful information to enrich your everyday life, Quarto Knows is a favorite destination for those pursuing their interests and passions. Visit our site and dig deeper with our books into your area of interest: Quarto Creates, Quarto Cooks, Quarto Homes, Quarto Lives, Quarto Drives, Quarto Explores, Quarto Gifts, or Quarto Kids.

This edition published in 2019 by Motorbooks, an imprint of The Quarto Group, 100 Cummings Center, Suite 265D, Beverly, MA 01915 USA.
T (978) 282-9590 F (978) 283-2742
www.QuartoKnows.com

Motorbooks titles are also available at discount for retail, wholesale, promotional, and bulk purchase. For details, contact the Special Sales Manager by email at specialsales@quarto.com or by mail at The Quarto Group, Attn: Special Sales Manager, 100 Cummings Center, Suite 265D, Beverly, MA 01915 USA.

10 9 8 7 6 5 4 3 2 1

ISBN: 978-0-7603-6341-6

Acquiring Editor: Zack Miller

On the front cover: 1967 Chevrolet Corvette Sting Ray. *Photo by Joseph Puhy*

Printed in China

For those who have driven, and those who will.
May the road deliver.

CONTRIBUTORS

ZACH BOWMAN has covered the automotive industry since 2007 as a writer and editor for a variety of outlets in print and online. His work has appeared in *Road & Track, Autoblog, Autoweek*, and *Automobile Magazine*. He hails from a family of the engine obsessed, with interests ranging from International Harvesters to classic Mercedes-Benzes. He currently serves as a contributing editor to *Cycle World* and *Motorcyclist* and resides in Lexington, Virginia, with his perpetually patient wife, Beth, and daughter, Lucy June.

LARRY WEBSTER oversees Hagerty's magazine, website, videos, and podcasts. He's been obsessed with cars and telling stories for decades. Before joining Hagerty, Webster was the editor-in-chief of *Road & Track*. He is an amateur race car driver who has competed on more than a dozen of North America's premier circuits and is a serial collector of vintage cars, which he restores in his home shop. Webster has a mechanical engineering degree from Lehigh University.

JACK BARUTH is a native New Yorker who long ago moved to rural Ohio and became a fervent evangelist for the Midwest perspective. He made his print debut at the age of 19 with *Bicycles Today* magazine before switching to four-wheeled topics. His work has been translated into more than a dozen languages, and he has stood on podiums in 14 different cycling and motorsports series, from New Jersey Motorsports Park to the Sepang International Circuit. He is an alumnus of several state institutions, not all of them educational.

BRETT BERK writes about the intersection of cars and culture. His work has appeared in an almost unconscionably diverse range of outlets, including *Autoweek, Billboard, Bloomberg Businessweek, Car and Driver, CNN, Departures, Details, Elle Decor, Entrepreneur, Esquire*, the *Globe and Mail, GQ*, the *Los Angeles Times, Maxim, Men's Health, Men's Journal*, the *New York Times, Popular Mechanics, Road & Track, Travel + Leisure, Vanity Fair, Vogue, Wired*, and *Yahoo!* He lives in New York City.

The Commitment BY ZACH BOWMAN

Peace in the Wrenches BY LARRY WEBSTER

The Joy of Driving BY JACK BARUTH

The Life BY BRETT BERK

FOREWORD

THERE'S NEVER BEEN A BETTER TIME TO GO FOR A DRIVE. As a nation, we are chronically overstressed, overworked, and, judging by the mattress stores that are in every mall, not sleeping enough. Worse yet, our digital devices are consuming ever increasing chunks of what free time we have left. According to a report by *60 Minutes,* social media apps are now programming *us.* Activities that force us to engage with ourselves and the environment around us are needed more than ever. The more we're plugged in, the more we need to unplug. Study after study proves the restorative effect hobbies have on creativity and mental health. Many people are taking this to heart, doing things for themselves that for decades were done for them or enjoying old-school pursuits—brewing and distilling their own beverages, raising backyard chickens, forging knives, embracing analog products like fountain pens and vinyl records. There's a growing hunger for hands-on pursuits.

Might we suggest a spin in a four-wheeled escape pod?

Making the car a pursuit invites not just the freedom of the road but also the potential to connect with thousands of like-minded individuals, as well as the pleasure of simply caring for the machine. Further, there's the thrill of commanding an object that's a high point of human ingenuity and design. Every car represents an unbroken chain of human creativity that goes back centuries.

Ralph Gilles, head of design at Fiat Chrysler Automobiles, relayed a story from when he was in charge of bringing the next Viper to market. He got that gig soon after Chrysler declared bankruptcy in 2009 and merged with Fiat. The new CEO of FCA, Sergio Marchionne, saw the Viper as a distraction to the larger job of making mass-market cars. But Gilles and his small band fought to keep the program alive and shouldered the task with thin resources. That meant countless long nights

and weekends to design and engineer the new car. Finally, the Viper was ready to be unveiled at the New York auto show in 2012. As Gilles climbed into the car to drive it on stage, the relief and joy of having overcome all those obstacles finally came due. "I was in the car," he said, "wiping away tears and trying to compose myself." There's a picture of him on that stage kissing the Viper's fender. Try telling Gilles a car is an inanimate object.

The automobile is the perfect embodiment of what makes us human. We make things. And then we improve and start again in an endless string of mechanical and design evolution. The car offers a connection to our humanity and ourselves. The car—the act of driving, repairing, maintaining—drives out distraction and demands we be "present."

Many car folks have engaged in this type of activity without ever thinking of the stimulating and restorative effects. They just dig it. Cars can connect us to broader communities and experiences, to our souls.

Never Stop Driving shines light on why we find these machines so captivating, offering inspiration and validation and finally inviting those who are curious but haven't made the leap to get into the car.

Let's roll.

—*Larry Webster*

PART ONE | BY **ZACH BOWMAN**

The Commitment

CARS INVITE PASSION.
PLENTY HAVE SHOWN THE WAY IN—BOTH HOW AND WHY.

1 / THE DEBATE

FOR MOST OF US, a vehicle is the second-largest purchase we'll make, topped only by a home. Yet when it comes to buying a car, practicality often takes a back seat to desire. Fuel economy and cargo space, crash ratings and emissions—none of that counts as much as how the machine makes us feel. It's why Corollas still come in red and why there are Audis and Acuras and Cadillacs when any old VW, Honda, or Chevy would do. Even in an age of automotive software updates and autonomy, in the face of a growing wave of generic transportation, cars matter.

That's not news for those of us who appreciate classics. Our enthusiasm for the cars we collect is an extension of the desire to drive something a little different, melded with the history, design, and ingenuity on display in an old machine. It's why we indulge ourselves with something so frivolous as a car bought for joy when life often demands our dollars elsewhere. These vehicles are beautiful and unique, imperfect and infuriating in equal measure, a mirror for our days.

This is not the realm of reason. To purchase, own, and drive a vintage car or truck or bike is to manifest enthusiasm in metal and glass. Those acts help us embrace the best parts of ourselves—the excited, curious, and gleeful bits that too many people abandon after childhood. The results are unquantifiable. You can't attach a dollar amount to catching a glint of autumn sun off the perfect arc of a fender, just as you can't to the happiness you get from food, drink, art, or song. Or, in my case, an abandoned '69 Triumph Spitfire. Finding, purchasing, fixing, and driving that tiny convertible was a perfect first immersion into the wide seas of vintage-car ownership.

It began with a flicker of an idea.

THE SPARK IS ALWAYS DIFFERENT. Maybe it's some scene from a film, the lead casting a sidelong glance through the passenger window before keying the ignition and driving off. It could be a tune, a forgotten refrain that waltzes through your mind, plucking memories from the shelves: the Camaro your uncle drove when he was young, the low chrome of your mother's Mercedes in the driveway, a summer afternoon in your own first car or the sweet evening that followed.

The inspiration to find a classic of your own can come from anywhere, but when it hits, it's unshakable. Years ago, I sold a 1971 Lincoln Continental Mark III and found myself with a conspicuous amount of garage space and a small pile of dollar bills. It's a dangerous, volatile combination, and in the interest of safety, I immediately set about rectifying the problem. But what to buy? It doesn't take a fortune to find and purchase an enjoyable vintage car. Even with my meager budget, the options were dizzying: domestic, European, Japanese? Truck, van, car? Hardtop or convertible? Sedan or coupe?

Sometimes it's easier to start by knowing what you don't want. The Lincoln was a massive American two-door, and I loved it. Actually, *love* is a strong word. It was a machine that had no problem deciding I was better off walking. It had a voracious appetite for leaded gasoline and physical space, devouring precious garage square footage like a Dearborn-bred black hole. For a decade, my wife and I squeezed around its wide flanks any time we entered or left the house, raising grocery bags over its swept rear deck as if we were fording a creek. I spent long hours chasing vacuum lines, trying to keep that massive engine from overheating. I pushed it, by myself, into gas stations and work bays. Heaving that car's 5000 pounds, even over flat ground, took everything my spindly writer legs could muster. By the time I signed the title over to the new owner, I knew I wanted something small and simple. Preferably with a number of cylinders countable on one hand.

I started looking around, flicking through online images, staring at old advertisements from decades before I was born. Here, a young couple posing by a hubcap-clad Datsun 510. There, a young lady taunting a man in a Porsche 914 with a snowball. I'd throw phrases into search engines and see what came back: Cortina, Lotus, Mini; Porsche, Datsun, Alfa. I didn't know it, but I was working toward an inevitability, the flowering of a seed planted when I couldn't have been more than five or six years old.

We were living in Knoxville then, my father, stepmother, and I, in a subdivision called Holiday Hills. It was a charmingly optimistic place, with exotic-sounding street names designed to evoke far-flung vacations. Ours was Aloha Avenue, and we shared it with our neighbor Bobby. I don't remember much about the guy. He had an awesome VHS collection, complete with every *Indiana Jones, Ghostbusters,* and *Star Wars* film produced to date. He liked plants and small dogs, and we'd water his collections of each when he traveled on business. But above all, he drove a pale yellow Fiat spider.

I don't actually remember ever seeing him in the car. The Fiat seemed to spend most of its time in our driveway with Dad under the hood, poking and prodding at something in exchange for a beer or two and conversation. One day in the garage, as I lurked nearby, Bobby looked at Dad. "Hey," he said, "why don't you sell this car for me?"

Even then, years from being able to legally own a vehicle, I wanted it. There was something in the Fiat's shape—different not just from everything else on the road, but from the bruising muscle cars I knew from Saturdays wandering car shows and junkyards with my father and uncle. It was penned in a different language. Delicate but masculine. The round headlights and the smiling grille made the car look friendly, but it wasn't goofy or awkward like a Miata. The low, thin windshield looked like an afterthought.

As far as I could tell, the car had no purpose. Not like our economical little Nissan pickup or Dad's disposable, commuter-spec Mustang. That made the Fiat *cool*.

Bobby must have been in sales. His idea of Dad's selling his spider for him was for my father to keep the car and drive it all summer, likely in the hope that it would find a home next door. We drove it everywhere, the top permanently down, Dad and my stepmother in the front seats and me wedged behind. It all seemed blissfully far from trouble, as if the universe had shifted chords from minor to major for a few moments. My memories of my father at his happiest are of right then, on a ride from dinner on a humid Tennessee night, with a handful of stars shining through the streetlights and nothing in the air but his wife's hair and the sound of a carbureted four-cylinder.

We did not buy the Fiat. Dad did as promised, selling the car to a stranger. Although Dad seemed pleased with his seller's fee, I took the spider's departure as a loss. It was my first taste of the grief that goes with missing a machine.

When my Lincoln went, I thought about that little Fiat. And the more I thought about that Italian roadster, the more I wanted something like it. I wanted to spend long Sunday afternoons driving through the Smoky Mountains with my wife. I wanted to bop downtown for lunch and leave the top open without a care. I wanted to own something beautifully purposeless. Of all the automotive permutations out there, of all the options then open to me, I settled on one specific vein: a small European convertible.

But that's like saying you love the color green. What shade? This is where it gets fun. I started keeping a mental list of the machines that might scratch my newfound itch. Most of the options hung out in the same era as that lost Fiat. I started seeing them everywhere—TR3s and TR4s, Alfa Graduates, 914s, Sprites, and Midgets. What about a Sunbeam? A Beetle? I wondered which one would look best parked in my empty garage.

I needed to have an honest conversation with myself about how I was going to use the car. I had visions of lazy road trips, but the reality was that neither my wife nor I had time to peel off and ramble the country. More likely, we'd pry loose a Sunday morning for blasts up the nearby Blue Ridge Parkway, never farther from home than a reasonable tow bill. That meant things like trunk space, range, and highway capability were less important. It meant I could entertain the idea of a car with more character than reliability.

Figuring out your own requirements might take a little more detective work. Experience often helps narrow the field, but it doesn't have to be *your* experience. Can you fold your six-foot frame into a Giulia? How stiff is the clutch in a Spitfire? It wasn't so long ago that answering those questions meant finding a car to physically drive. Now it's as easy as finding a group of owners online, introducing yourself, and asking. On top of that, 100 test drives could never tell you if a car is cold-natured or prone to overheating, or if the wipers can do more than just rest handsomely on the windshield. Never in the history of the human race has research been so easy—or enthusiasts so willing to share information.

My days took on a predictable pattern. I'd see something intriguing in traffic and then fall into a fit of forum scouring, blowing my lunch hour reading about Porsche rust repair and British Leyland overdrive units. I'd stop drivers at gas stations to chat about the reliability of their inherently unreliable loves. In doing so, I found something surprising: No one told me to take a hike. Of the many people I pounced on with questions, every last one took the time to share what he or she knew. Some even offered to let me drive their cars, although I politely declined. They seemed to be made of time, and I envied that. Those people weren't out in their classic because they had somewhere to go. They were exactly where they wanted to be, doing what they wanted to do, enjoying a machine and sharing that joy with a complete stranger.

That knowledge made it easier to haunt car shows, too. It can be intimidating to approach someone at an organized gathering. Owners typically cluster, chatting about paint codes and parts finds, but most car-show participants are there to share and won't mind a few questions. Think of those sprawling parking lots and fields as libraries. There's no better place to get a feel for the cars you're considering than at a show, where vehicles are real and in motion, not simply images on a screen.

Part of my research was discovering what I thought I could tolerate. Notice I didn't say "we." My wife, Beth, has always been made of sterner stuff than I. She has perfected a particularly communicative raised eyebrow to indicate that my caterwauling is excessive for the suffering at hand. I chalk this up to her parents, saints who carried her through childhood in a long line of nearly dead sedans and minivans. In high school, she drove a battered Honda Accord with a fourth cylinder that

inexplicably fouled plugs by the pack. She bought them by the gross, and she could have a dead one out and a new one in quicker than I could figure out how to pop the hood. Beth didn't care what I found, as long as I quit badgering her with what-ifs.

I lived in Tennessee at the time, a place blessed with seasons in equal helpings. There were reasonably cold winters and hot, muggy summers. Did I need a functional heater? I'm not one to park a car for winter, preferring instead to spend a chilly but sunny day with the top down. Heat was a must. How about air-conditioning? I'd prized the A/C in the Lincoln, mostly because the car's dark green paint and green leather turned it into a cruel oven when the thermometer climbed above 60. But with a convertible? Why bother?

There was a larger question: What condition was I shopping for? My budget immediately precluded concours perfection, but a solid, handsome driver was within reach. My problem is that squared-away usable vehicles have never held as much allure as spending twice as much building a shade of the same. At this point in my life, it's become a pattern. (Sometimes I wonder if Beth married me more out of scientific curiosity than anything else.)

Your criteria will hinge on what you're comfortable with. If you're keen on learning, a vintage car can be a great way to familiarize yourself with basic mechanical work. Cars that came before the age of the microprocessor are vignettes of the human capacity for cleverness, a collection of solutions to the 1000 questions that can arise on a given journey. Discovering those brilliant answers on your own time is a sharp joy. Prying the why from something as simple as a door hinge is like unlocking a code. It's a link to the minds and hands that wrestled with suspension geometry and piston-skirt length, grinding out their days by paycheck or passion decades before the machine wandered into your life. It's the human whisper behind every set of headlights.

This was, and remains, my sucker punch. Despite my cursing, I had enjoyed tinkering with the Lincoln. One evening, after the car had issued a rare flawless performance as our ride downtown for dinner, I nosed it into the garage and shut off the engine. Naturally, the Lincoln

1964 Pontiac Tempest LeMans GTO. *Photo by Andrew Trahan*

1970 Datsun 1600. *Photo by DW Burnett*

refused to start the next day. Nothing about it made any sense. We'd just spent hours without even a miss in the V-8's easy gait. I sat in the wide leather front seat, my hands wrapped around the thin wheel. That mammoth machine barely fit in the garage. Getting in and out was like playing fat-man squeeze—because the thing was longer than a Chevrolet Suburban, I always parked with its pointed nose inches from the back wall. The long doors opened only so wide before getting cozy with a toolbox or door.

This all meant there was no simple way to roll the car backward. I spent a week shimmying around fenders and sitting awkwardly on the radiator support. I poked and prodded, checking the usual suspects. I replaced a cracked coil, examined plugs and fuel flow, removed and cleaned the carburetor. None of it worked.

It's strange how easy we tend to make our lives. Adolescence is a series of seemingly impossible goals requiring struggle, learning, and self-expansion. But as adults, we surround ourselves with a galaxy of tools designed to reduce mental or physical load. As infuriating as an obstinate big-block can be, it's a stern and patient teacher. In a moment of peak exasperation, I placed a hand on the distributor to steady myself. It turned freely. The locking bolt had backed out just enough to allow the distributor to twist. In that moment, I could see what happened as clearly as if the car had drawn a picture: When I shut the engine off that night after dinner, the force of the car's internals coming to a stop had nudged the distributor in its housing. Since the distributor's position helps set ignition timing, this made sense. The timing had shifted just enough to keep the engine from firing.

I wanted to cry. Or laugh. Or jump around and shout my idiot victory until the neighbors called the police. Instead, I adjusted the timing, tightened the bolt, started the car, and went for a drive. Now any time a machine stops unexpectedly, I check the distributor first.

Of course, most sane people want to spend most of their time with a car driving it, not writhing around in the garage. Again, honesty is essential here: What do you want out of ownership? Self-discovery and edification are great, but they won't mean much if you wind up with a project that spirals out of control and never sees the road. Most of us know someone who has a derelict stuffed in a corner somewhere. Speaking from experience, that's a miserable place to be. If you're uncertain about your own ability or desire to tackle mechanical work, finding a sorted vehicle is a safer bet. Old cars always require attention, and some need more than others.

As for me, I hadn't narrowed my search at all. I eyed everything from complete basket cases, panels in piles and pistons in boxes, to glossy drivers that needed only a tank of fuel. It went on like that for months as I ticked off mental boxes, slowly working toward a solution. Sometimes, however, the right answer finds you. Mine did.

When I sat behind the wheel,
everything seemed to fit. The low doorsills
held my arm and guided my hand
to the massive spoked steering wheel.
It wasn't perfect, but neither was I.

1956 Porsche 356A Carrera 1500GS. *Photo by Amy Shore*

2 / THE HUNT

WHEN I WAS A KID, my uncle Fred used to say, "They all look good from the road." I didn't grasp what he meant until years later, after I'd made all the mistakes he had stumbled through during his years of buying and selling vintage Chevrolets. These days, we compare the marks of our lessons and laugh. There was the time he drove to Orlando to purchase a Suburban, only to have the fuel pump die a mile from the seller. Or the old International I bought from a biker who had hocked the title for a grand. The era is immaterial; Fred's seven words serve as sage advice, pocket wisdom that holds everything anyone needs to know about buying an older vehicle.

Uncle Fred found his cars through papers like the *Thrifty Nickel* and *PennySaver,* scrounging through tersely worded classifieds. Or he found them while driving county four-lanes, scanning for windshields painted with "FOR SALE" and a phone number. He'd pull into strange driveways after traveling for half a day, knocking on doors, hoping to be greeted by a warm smile and not the twin black holes of a 12-gauge. He brought home a long line of beautiful cars this way, including a Top Flight 1971 Corvette and four of the five C/10 pickups that it took to build his '72 short-bed.

At first, I thought he was talking about distance. From the safety of a photo or highway, a car for sale exists in the theoretical. It builds a pretty little life in your head. It is the low-mile, never-seen-rain unicorn you've been searching for. It will start with a breath on the key and ferry you across the continent untroubled. It is priced thousands below market value. The fantasy sprawls on in the brief moments before you act on your find. You see yourself and your spouse in the front seat,

1954 Chevrolet Corvette.
Photo by Ben Woodworth

sharing some private laugh as a parade builds around you, people applauding your good sense as you drive past. Confetti falls. World peace follows.

THEN THE IMAGE FALLS APART. You get close and see tobacco-sack floorboards and a body by Bondo. Few dreams hold up to reality—that was true 40 years ago, when Uncle Fred was buying and selling cars, and it's true now, when the majority of vintage-vehicle classifieds exist online.

You have to let your optimism do the shopping and let your skepticism write the check.

With the buying and selling of old cars, as with most things, the internet has expanded our options exponentially. The upsides are obvious: There are few joys as bright as swapping classified links with buddies via e-mail or text, collectively drooling over some piece of forbidden fruit at the far end of the country. There have always been dealers who specialize in classic cars, but their wares are now accessible in seconds. Likewise, nearly every forum has a classified section full of vehicles owned by knowledgeable people. Finally, sites like Autotrader Classics, Craigslist, eBay, Bring a Trailer, and Facebook Marketplace all offer a buffet of vintage metal. The end result is that a careful buyer can acquire a vehicle from 5000 miles away as easily as from five miles down the road.

The operative word there is careful. We can't discuss purchasing a used vehicle of any sort without acknowledging the predatory sellers who lurk in the shadows. The vintage market seems particularly fraught with individuals who, at best, claim their vehicle is something it isn't. At worst, they hope to abscond to the Caribbean with your bank information. None of which is to say you should sit at home clutching your wallet to your chest. As with any purchase, it pays to have your wits about you. The good news is, it's easy to protect yourself from becoming a scam victim and from bringing home a car that's more headache than heartthrob.

First, know where you're shopping. Although relatively anonymous listing services like Craigslist, Facebook Marketplace, and Autotrader allow anyone to sell anything, they offer little accountability. Sellers don't have a reputation to uphold past their own honor. That's not the case with sites like eBay and Bring a Trailer that work to vet sellers and will outright ban anyone they deem detrimental to the community. Likewise, a good forum will work to weed out abusive members. That hardly means everyone in such an environment is a choir-singing Boy Scout, but it's something to keep in mind.

TO BORROW AN OLD SAW, the best defense against a predatory seller is a good offense. Predatory sellers rely on a buyer's desire for a good deal, and they craft situations that make you think you've discovered a gem. Above all, beware absurdly low asking prices. By the time you're ready to pull the trigger on a purchase, you'll have a good idea of a car's ballpark value. Great deals exist, but the internet has helped make them increasingly rare. (Just as you have access to an incredible amount of information, so do most sellers.) Above all, be prepared to walk away if anything seems strange or out of place: sellers who will only communicate via e-mail, for example, or who refuse to answer specific questions. Pay attention to listing details, too. If the vehicle is for sale in Montana, why is the car parked in front of palm trees in the photos? Has the description been lifted from Wikipedia? Does the seller's area code match his or her claimed location? At this stage, your gut is your best ally.

All of this applies wherever you chase your vehicle. Many of Uncle Fred's tried and true classifieds still exist, and they can yield amazing finds. Most local newspapers still feature a classified section, *Hemmings Motor News* is still an industry pillar, and almost every classic-car club boasts a newsletter with special-interest ads. Just remember: The internet didn't invent the scam; it just gave it a new playground.

Once you've made contact with the seller, don't be afraid to ask for a first and last name. Those two pieces of information, along with a phone number or e-mail address, can be plugged into a search engine and produce a shocking amount of information. You can discover if an individual has ever had a brush with the law or been sued in civil court for fraud. If you're purchasing from a dealer, you can scour online reviews and check in with the local Better Business Bureau. No one piece of information can tell you if a listing is legitimate, but the composite can give you an idea of how gun-shy to be.

Regardless of where you find your vehicle, it helps to know what's normal. Good sellers will answer any questions you have with clarity and honesty. They'll happily discuss the car on the phone, take any additional photos you request, and have no trouble meeting you or a representative for a thorough examination. They should also have no problem allowing you to take the vehicle for a test drive, within reason. Some sellers might ask for a deposit in hand, or proof of insurance in the event the unfortunate happens while you're lapping the block. They might also want to ride along with you. That's all normal.

Even with this knowledge, however, there's no substitute for humanity. Shortly after I graduated from college, a friend called, excited about the car he'd just brought home. Donny had been searching for a C3 Corvette for months and had finally found one within his budget: a 1973, burgundy with black interior. He bought it on the spot.

"It's perfect," he said. "You have to see it the next time you're in town."

Perfect it was not. When I first put eyes on it, the Corvette was sitting in a dimly lit mechanic's shop, gremlins plaguing the ignition system. Even under the flickering fluorescents, the paint appeared to have been applied by garden hose. A quick peek underneath revealed jagged holes in the frame larger than the windows in my first apartment. He looked at me optimistically.

"What do you think?"

I didn't have the heart to tell him he'd succumbed to a few vintage-car-shopping pitfalls. The seller had been less than honest, for one thing, claiming the car was a clean, unmolested example. Donny, being young, relatively inexperienced, and alone, had taken the guy's word

1973 Dodge Dart Swinger.

1972 AMC Ambassador.
Photos by DW Burnett

32

for it, paid the asking price, and driven home. This is a man who's had a clear path for his life laid out since we were kids. While the rest of us were squandering small fortunes in college, trying to see how many beer cans we could stack in a dorm window, he was already well on his way to securing a navy pension as a nuclear engineer, ensuring that our nation's atomic-powered aircraft carriers didn't glow green in the night. Why would he, of all people, do such a thing?

The lesson here is to never go it alone. A second set of eyes is invaluable with any vehicle purchase, more so when the car is a classic. Maybe it's a friend who knows a bit about the model in question, or maybe it's just a skeptical spouse who will zero in on the wavy bodywork and leaky weatherstripping that you're too smitten to see. In a perfect situation, that second set of eyes belongs to a genuine expert, someone qualified to give a prepurchase inspection, or PPI. Regardless of where you live, a master in whatever make and model you fancy is never far away, and a good shop will trade a modest fee for a few hours going over your dream purchase. It's cheap insurance.

But Donny fell victim to more than a dishonest seller. Something strange happens after you've spent a few weeks searching for the car of your dreams. Your lizard brain, tired of weighing pros and cons, shoves your rational self out of the way and grabs the wheel. Suddenly, when a car comes along—any car—you lock onto it, damn the torpedoes. It's shopping fatigue, no different from the kind you feel at the mall or the grocery store. But instead of bringing home a tie two inches too long or a shopping cart full of nothing but canned pineapple, you wind up with a Corvette well on its way to becoming a natural reef.

The feeling can arise for all sorts of reasons: boredom, impatience, anxiety. You start believing there simply aren't that many of your desired vehicle in existence, that all the good ones already have loving homes. In that moment, take a breath. Unless you're buying a one-of-one exotic, the car you're hunting likely exists by the hundreds, if not thousands. There might not be a plethora of them near you at that given moment, but there's no telling what will come up in a week, or a month, or six months.

In other words, be patient. All cars are commodities. Most were mass-produced. Nothing's so rare as to warrant putting yourself in the unfortunate position of paying to possess a nightmare.

When Donny saw my pained expression, he lifted the sagging driver's door into place, latching it closed.

"It needs a little work," he said, "but it'll be great when it's done."

Of his many missteps, that thinking was the clincher. What wouldn't be great with $10,000 of body work, another $8000 in paint, and a fully rebuilt driveline? It's so easy to be dismissive of a vehicle's problems when you're in the moment, when your reptile self is in control and ready to make any move that frees you from the hunt. Everything is fixable, but purchase day is the day to weigh every flaw in heart and wallet. How much will that dinged quarter-panel cost to correct? Will a paintless dent repair take care of it, or will you have to find a qualified body shop? Is that oil leak a valve-cover gasket or a rear main seal?

Remember: You aren't auditioning for the role of the car's owner. You're interviewing the machine. If something feels off, there's zero shame in walking away. Donny did a bit of work on his '73, and he later sold it for close to what he'd paid. In the pantheon of expensive lessons, he got off easy.

It wasn't shopping fatigue that got me, however. It was the car itself. The ad showed the remains of a '69 Triumph Spitfire. The front bumper and hood were punched in, the grille and most of the interior missing. The rear quarter was smashed behind the driver's door. Optimism told me to go take a look. The seller was a nice guy, honest about the car's history. He was a full-blown British-car nut, his shop packed with Sprites and other Triumphs. The Spit sat in the back corner. He'd purchased it from the original owner, he said. He told me all about every dent and ding, how someone in an old F-150 had backed into the car's nose after not seeing it in a parking lot, the truck's trailer hitch putting deep gouges in the sheetmetal; how less than a month later the same thing had happened on the driver's side, an F-150 again. Then he uttered a version of that famous phrase:

"It ran when we parked it back there."

The Spitfire wore tags from the year before I was born. The top was gone, and the seats were in tatters. It needed everything: brakes and tires, belts and hoses, every fluid. The radiator showed obvious signs of leaking. It was far from a driver, but it was also surprisingly whole. Spitfires aren't known for their rust resistance, but this one still wore its factory floor pans, trunk pan, and rockers. Only the battery tray showed some corrosion. All the glass was intact, and the factory wiring harness was complete. When I dug around under the seats, I found the previous owner's calculus homework from the University of Tennessee, along with a couple of #2 pencils. It looked as if she had simply parked the vehicle at some point during the Reagan administration and never bothered to start it again.

The current owner was kind enough to allow me to examine the car as thoroughly as I liked. He clearly wasn't trying to hide anything. The engine had compression, the clutch disengaged, and the shift lever went through all the gears. Both SU carburetors were mounted on the intake, dirty but intact. Neither the oil nor the coolant showed signs of a blown head gasket.

More important, I wanted the car. Under the dull paint and dented panels sat a gorgeous little thing, one of the last undiluted British roadsters from the age before federal regulations forced goofy bumpers on everything. When I sat behind the wheel, everything seemed to fit. The low doorsills held my arm and guided my hand to the massive spoked steering wheel. The wooden shift knob filled my palm, and big Jaeger gauges gazed back at me from the dash. It wasn't perfect, but neither was I. I figured we'd get along fine, the two of us figuring each other out over the next few months. I'd never driven a Spitfire, and I knew it would be weeks before I would get the car to turn a tire, but damn the torpedoes, the mouse droppings, and entropy. It felt right.

I made the seller an offer. He agreed to my price on the condition that I also take a second parts car he had lurking in the back lot, another $500. I agreed, as long as he'd foot the bill for the rollback that brought the two Spits to my place across town.

We shook hands, and just like that, my hunt was over. The cars showed up at the house on a bright spring afternoon, the sky a shock of blue that promised longer, warmer days. Convertible weather.

Even the Pros Make Mistakes

BY COLIN COMER

I've bought and sold hundreds of cars over the past 33 years. No, probably thousands. But don't let the sheer number of transactions fool you, as it was bolstered by many years of being a late-model used-car dealer. Nevertheless, I think I have enough deals under my belt to know one thing: It doesn't matter how many or what kind of cars you buy, there isn't one of us who hasn't screwed up at least once. Or, in my case, far more than once. As much as I'd like to think it won't happen again, I know it will. And that's okay, because professional or not, it's all a part of the game.

I was first burned on the second car I bought. I was 13 years old. It was a 1970 MG B/GT I found advertised in a *PennySaver* while having dinner with my dad, the British car fan, who decided we should go see it right away. We met the seller, John Smith, after dark at the address he gave, a nice ranch home in Sheboygan, Wisconsin. In the garage were two mint 1966 Dodge Chargers. In the driveway sat the B/GT. It was in gray primer, described by Mr. Smith as a stalled project his son was working on and all it needed was paint. It ran well, and the interior was decent. My dad and I both deemed Mr. Smith a nice, honest fellow and bought the car for $900. When we picked it up the next day, it didn't look as good as it did in the dark, but a deal is a deal. My dad questioned why the title wasn't in Mr. Smith's name, but apparently, the explanation was good enough. The drive home was when it got interesting. It was a pretty windy ride, likely because the plywood and garbage bags that comprised the "floor" soon gave way. When we stopped for gas, very little fuel stayed in the rusty tank. Yet ignorance and 13-year-old optimism are bliss, so we soldiered on. Once we got the B/GT home, I started to poke around the old gal. Beyond the nonexistent floors, there wasn't much left of the rocker panels, fenders, or quarter-panels, either. Kind of a problem for a unibody car, I might add. Covering the decay were aftermarket fiberglass body panels crudely fastened by blind rivets and covered in rattle-can primer. My "only needs a coat of paint" sports car became my first ground-up restoration. Some months later, I saw Mr. Smith at the local hardware store when I was restocking on Bondo. I called across the aisles saying, "Hi, Mr. Smith." He didn't reply. Only then did I connect the dots. It was my first exposure to a "flipper" using an alias.

To this day I contend that no Ivy League education can hold a candle to the one I got for $900. But even the best education won't make you bullet-proof. Identifying flippers, rust, and poor mechanical condition is one aspect. As the years went on and collector cars gained value rapidly, fraud did as well. When I started to trade in higher-dollar muscle cars, I was shocked at how good forgers were and the lengths some people would go to deceive. Thankfully, being cautious helped me avoid getting skinned, but there were a few times I ended up buying cars sight unseen during the crazy days of 2004–7 that weren't all they were cracked up to be. Why? Sometimes you had to roll the dice or risk losing a car that could be a winner. And it isn't always the sellers doing the con. Sometimes they were sold a bill of goods, and you're just next in line.

One of these instances was when I bought a rare 1970 Challenger R/T convertible from a local collector. Restored like jewelry, it had been in multiple magazines and on the cover of a book, and it had won high-level awards from all the right shows. Sublime green with a white interior and factory A/C, it was a real knockout. I had to have it. Represented as having its numbers-matching engine, I inspected the car in the seller's immaculate garage, and sure enough, lying under the car with a flashlight, I could see that the proper date code, casting number, and correct VIN were on the block. I knew I was at the front of a long line of people who wanted it if I passed. It was a put-up or shut-up moment in the super-heated Mopar E-body market at the time. Pass, and I might never get another chance at a car like this for anywhere near the price. So rather than put the car under the microscope, I wrote a check on the spot. I bought the car and drove it for a few years. When I decided to sell it, the buyer, inspecting the car on my hoist, asked if I could clean the paint off the VIN on the engine block so he could

Comer's 1970 Dodge Challenger R/T convertible.
Photo by Colin Comer

read it better. Moments later I was witnessing lead shavings coming off the blade of my pocketknife, along with the VIN stamp. It seems the restorer had used a replacement block, ground out the original numbers, poured molten lead into the depression, and then stamped the correct VIN into the lead and painted it all pretty. The buyer still wanted the car, but a significant price reduction ended up being a part of the deal. Another degree earned—this one a master's in "act in haste, repent at leisure."

It's easier to get a lesson buying a car at auction, since you need to rely on the catalog or the owner's description, and I've learned a few of those as well: a 10,000-original-mile Camaro that ended up being 110,000 when I started searching out previous owners; a number of cars reported to "drive like new" in the auction copy that hardly made it from the auction parking lot to my trailer—including an original 427 Cobra restored by a known high-profile shop that failed to make anything work or even balance the rebuilt engine. Actually, the number of cars I've bought at auction that were truly mechanically fit are far outnumbered by the ones that weren't. I always factor some amount of money for the stuff I can't check out before raising my hand to the auctioneer.

I've also had my share of title problems. A photo or copy of the title won't always tell the full story, because there could be a duplicate title or a hidden lien, or the title might have been improperly assigned. Some previous sellers might have skipped the title step altogether. Any of these scenarios could end with you, the new buyer, holding a nonnegotiable title for a car, which is a pain to correct. The last problem title I had took eight months to straighten out—for a $15,000 car.

In the end, these negative experiences pale in comparison to the good ones. For every bum deal, I've had a dozen great ones and gotten cars I loved. I look at these few bad deals as simply a side effect of doing something I love. I don't golf, but I'm sure people who do view country club memberships and greens fees the same way. High-stakes gamblers don't love a bad night at the table, and a pilot might view maintenance costs and hangar fees as a necessary evil of getting above the clouds. The best advice I can give is take your time, do as much due diligence as you can, and if a deal still ends up not being ideal, don't let it ruin your enjoyment of the car or the hobby. Even the best of us get excited and go off-script once in a while, but try not to lose sight of the target. We're here to have fun, and buying and selling cars is a large part of that. For better or for worse.

Colin Comer is the founder of Colin's Classic Automobiles, the author of several best-selling automotive books, a noted collector, and the chief judge of the Milwaukee Concours d'Elegance. He remains a hopeless romantic when it comes to old cars, despite the few he wishes he'd never bought.

3 / YOU HAVE THE CAR—NOW WHAT?

THERE IS NO MANUAL for the mountain of quirks that can come with a vintage car or truck. These vehicles are so far removed from the anonymous, effortless automobiles we know today that it takes some time to adjust to the way things were. There's real satisfaction in learning the secret handshake required to start your car in February and the different moves it takes to do the same in June, coaxing the vehicle alive with the right dance of fuel, choke, and starter. There's some aggravation at having to sprint around a vehicle to unlock a passenger door in the rain because it was built before the advent of central locking. Two sides to every coin.

The first few months are like the early days of any relationship. There's a lot of bliss—moments when you throw open the garage door and marvel at what's sitting there. There's also bound to be some misery. Every bit of it is fun in one way or another, either in the moment or long after when you're sharing the story with friends and family.

Before you get to any of that, take the time to do a solid preflight check. Make certain your tires, including the spare, have the appropriate air pressure and the oil and transmission fluid are at the level they should be. The first month or two of ownership should be dedicated to giving your new-to-you car a maintenance baseline, changing the fluids and generally discovering what's been taken care of and what hasn't. It's a time for you or your mechanic to get to know the vehicle so you have some idea of its mechanical health and what might need attention in the coming months.

Getting the Spitfire up off its heels took less time than I'd wagered. Parts were easy to find and relatively inexpensive, and high-dollar items

Uncovering the mysteries of a new project. *Photo by Steve Cucinotta*

like the fuel tank and radiator were easily repaired by local shops. I spent three weeks waiting for my carburetors to come back from a restoration specialist. When they arrived, I didn't want to hide them under the hood. Their dashpots shone like new, and paired with a few other engine upgrades, they had the car singing.

Even so, the Spit had slumbered for decades, and I had no idea why the original owner had parked it. Was there some terrible engine failure lurking in my future? Maybe the transmission was on the verge of firing the output shaft from its case like a metal pimple. I hadn't spent enough time with the machine to know whether I could trust it to take me across town and back, let alone on that perfect fall drive I'd dreamed of all those months before.

I finished up the major work a few days shy of our first wedding anniversary. Feeling particularly pleased with myself, I bolted in a pair of brand-new lapbelts and suggested to Beth that we take the Spit to dinner. She beamed from the passenger seat, her long hair catching the sun as I shifted into fourth. We didn't make it more than a mile before the car started stuttering.

Beth's look changed to one of tolerant bemusement as we rolled to a standstill. I couldn't believe it—I had made something like a dozen laps around the block in the preceding week, doing my best to make certain the car was up to this very task. I checked those big, beautiful Jaegers. The engine temperature was perfect. The fuel gauge read full up. When I hit the key, the starter leapt to life. Power clearly wasn't a problem.

After 10 minutes of checking every other potential culprit, I popped the filler lid and stared down into the fuel tank. It was bone dry. The three gallons I'd poured in to tune the carburetors had long since been sent floating into the Tennessee air.

Like all relationships, the one you have with a vintage vehicle is built on trust, and trust only manifests itself with time and experience. We're accustomed to believing everything our modern vehicles tell us, from our location to temperature, time of day, and tire pressure. Old gauges are famously full of mischief, and they can lead to far worse problems than pushing your wife and your fuel-starved Spitfire a mile home on your anniversary. Then again, nothing says, "I love you," like shoving a 1500-pound convertible down a country two-lane on a Tennessee June afternoon. A good first step with any new purchase is to find out exactly which gauges are telling the truth and which ones are waiting to yank the rug out from under you.

After that, the easiest way to get to know a car is to use it. One of the mistakes buyers make is treating their vintage vehicles like museum pieces, locking them away in dark garages in the hope of preserving them forever or in fear of damaging them. All vehicles exist under a universal truth: They are machines, and machines are made to be used and enjoyed. What's more, nothing is so damaging to a vehicle as being stationary. Seals harden or break down and begin to leak, gasoline goes stale, brake calipers lock in place, and clutches corrode shut. Just as your muscles will atrophy if you sit still for months, so too will a machine wither with inactivity. The more you drive the car, the healthier it will be, and the more familiar you'll become with its language of squeaks and rattles. Before long, you'll know what's normal and what might signal serious mechanical trouble.

Start small. Instead of taking your Camry to the coffee shop on Saturday morning, take your classic. Drive it to the office on Friday or to the next town over for dinner with friends. In short, don't be afraid to stretch the machine's legs. When a breakdown does happen—if you drive long and far enough, that's inevitable—don't worry. Take the moment in stride, and use it as an excuse to correct whatever weak spot you managed to expose.

One day after work, I drove the Spit downtown, its maiden voyage past my neighborhood. It was the first time I'd had the car up to any real speed, and to my surprise, it felt great. Or rather, it felt as good as a 1969 Triumph with blown shocks and tired bushings could feel, which is to say, like a tower of damp cardboard boxes. But the little 1.3-liter four was bright and spunky, the transmission shifted beautifully, and the differential was as quiet as I could reasonably expect. After dinner with Beth and a few friends, I pointed the car toward home, taking the back way and enjoying a long, gorgeous sunset. The heat of the day had broken, and the first sweet breaths of cool night air came drifting through the trees as the streetlights flickered on. I was driving my dream for the first time since I began searching for the car, watching the orange lamps reflect in the chrome trim along each front fender as my hair blew in the wind.

Maybe you're seeing a pattern here. That's when the engine stumbled, then died altogether.

It's funny how feeling in the moment can outshout the voice of reason. I coasted into a nearby parking lot, certain that I'd sunk a valve or snapped the camshaft, that the engine was now a hunk of slag under the hood, all the money and time I'd spent on the car wasted. Would this be the limit of my wife's patience? When I finally drew the courage to pop the hood, I found that two of my brand-new spark-plug wires had simply popped off the distributor cap. I plugged them back in, and when I hit the key, the engine fired up, happy to carry us home.

Of all the tools to carry with you while enjoying your new classic, Occam's Razor might be the most important. Assuming the worst is a natural reaction to any circumstance, and it can help prepare you for what's coming your way. But in general, older machines are relatively simple, needing only a few ingredients to function. Breakdowns are rarely caused by massive mechanical trouble. It's usually some fiddly piece that needs a minor poke to get back in order, and you only learn what those bits are by using the machine. The next time it happens, you'll look like a hero when you, for example, pop the hood, snap your plug wires back in place, and drive on as if such a move is a perfectly normal activity for a Tuesday-morning commute.

Whether you're addressing the issue yourself or trusting it to a mechanic, it's important to define the scope of the work ahead of time. We've all heard the urban legends of people who took their car in for a wheel bearing and came out with a rotisserie restoration, three years and $60,000 later.

Although I've never had it that bad, I've certainly seen a project run amok. My 1978 International Scout Terra began as a high-school toy but devolved into an ongoing effort that spanned the better part of 12 years.

Old cars and the manuals that hold their secrets are trips through history. *Photos by Amy Shore (top) and Steve Cucinotta (bottom)*

By the time I sold the truck, I could count the original components on one hand. The top, the engine, the frame, a portion of the firewall, and the inside of the bed were all that remained of my original Scout, and when I was done, I was left with something that barely resembled the old Binder I'd fallen for as a kid.

It's easy to talk yourself into more work than is necessary, falling victim to "while you're in there" syndrome: replacing everything you see because you've gained access to it, not because you need to. But the smarter approach is to make safety issues the first priority, followed by reliability. Cosmetic and convenience problems can always wait if they get in the way of time behind the wheel. Save them for the bleak winter months, when dry, sunny days are few and far between and when your wallet has recovered from the original purchase. The great joy of a vintage car is its unnecessity. No problem can arise that, if it's not solved immediately, will keep you from getting to work on Monday.

What about treacherous parking lots full of buggies waiting to mangle your precious sheetmetal? What about cell-phone-wielding drivers, potholes, and pigeons with full digestive tracts? Don't fret the world's dangers at the expense of spending time with your vehicle. For one thing, the odds are in your favor. The universe doesn't often turn cruel toward our daily drivers, and those machines endure far greater exposure to the world's fangs than your classic ever will.

On top of this, and hard to believe, is the truth that vintage cars are some of humans' most forgiving creations. There's almost nothing on most classics that can't be rebuilt, re-created, or replaced. That's one of the true gifts of these machines and why so many mechanics find solace in them. They carry a certain immortality, immune to the wear of time and miles as long as an attentive owner is willing to do the work necessary to keep them alive. And yes, replacing original parts can be a detriment to the vehicle's value for some collectors, but for most people, cars aren't investment pieces.

You're better off thinking of a classic car like a bottle of wine—something to be savored and enjoyed with friends, not stored in a dusty cellar. None of this is to say your classic will be without limits, or that you should throw good money after bad—especially if, like my friend Donny, you find your resources in constant drain. At some point, my uncle Fred's '72 C/10 became that vehicle. He spent long hours going through that Chevy in a nuts-and-bolts restoration, hell-bent on making the truck into the ultimate version of itself. For a while, it was also undrivable. He'd set off for work only to have the big V-8 die within sight of the office, leaving him to walk the last half-mile. It became a running gag, the guys at work ribbing him for being so passionate about his exercise that he'd just leave "that nice truck parked anywhere."

Worse, Fred didn't feel comfortable putting anyone else in the passenger seat, for fear the pickup would lie down and strand them. When the C/10 began spending most of its time in the garage, he sent it on to a new owner, someone who was undoubtedly relieved to find that the Chevy looked as good up close as it did from the road.

Beth and I enjoyed the Spitfire throughout the summer, but the longer I spent with the car, the more I realized it wasn't what I had in mind at the beginning of my hunt. The nonsynchronized first gear was an aggravation, the transverse rear leaf spring helped the car corner like a wobbly egg, and a stereotypical host of electrical woes meant I spent nearly as much time wiggling wires as driving.

But the final straw had more to do with how I was using the car than any fault of its own. One Friday night after dinner, I sat in line in a downtown parking garage, waiting my turn to pay for parking and leave. A parked Suburban to my left started up and immediately began to reverse. I reached for the horn to let the driver know I was there—the same horn that had worked flawlessly from the moment I'd brought the car home.

No matter how hard I pressed the button, no sound came out. All the while, that Suburban's trailer hitch inched closer and closer to removing the Spitfire's windshield. The line of cars remained stopped, me locked in a perfect bumper-height blind spot behind the big Chevrolet. In a moment of desperation, I shouted a line of curses unfit for publication, the pitch and timber of which managed to pierce the big truck's laminated glass. The driver stopped about a

foot from the Triumph. Beth was in line behind me in our Subaru, and she watched the whole scene play out. To her great credit, she never said a word about it. It's not lost on me that she didn't bother blowing her horn, either.

We never took that gorgeous drive up the Blue Ridge Parkway. I put the Triumph up for sale a few weeks after that moment in the parking garage, just in time for the leaves to change and the east Tennessee weather to turn. In the end, the Spitfire and the parts car left us for about what we had in them, and I didn't feel too sour about it. I was never a Boy Scout, but I've always admired that organization's dedication to leaving things better than they found them. When the Triumph rolled into my shop, it was one bad day from the scrap heap. When it left, it was a fully functional vehicle, horn included. It felt good to watch the little car drive off down our road, heading into the future having escaped time's scythe for a little longer.

When and if it comes time for you to send your classic to a new home, nothing's more important than honesty and transparency, even if it means taking a few hundred dollars less than you'd like. On a basic level, it makes the hobby better for everyone. We all want to buy from someone who has nothing to hide, and the easiest way for that to happen is for there to be more honest sellers.

No one likes the thought of taking a bath on a purchase, but it pays to remember that your dollars bought more than the physical object sitting in your driveway. Every vintage vehicle I've owned has taught me more than all the hours I've spent combing the internet and flipping through service manuals. There's simply no substitute for spending time with a machine, for putting your hands on the wheel and gazing through a windshield that has watched the world change in ways no one could have predicted. Those experiences are part of the vocabulary of vintage vehicles, a shared experience with other owners, both living and passed. It's all hard to put a value on—to say nothing of the grins the machine gives you along the way.

PART TWO BY LARRY WEBSTER

Peace in the Wrenches

THE CHALLENGE OF A PROBLEM,
THE GLOW OF A SOLUTION,
THE LESSONS IN A TOOL BOX.

4/ LEFT, RIGHT, AND NO BRAIN

IF YOU LUST AFTER THE LATEST ALFA ROMEO, Jeep, or Ram pickup, then the guy standing in front of me, swinging a torque wrench, is who you have to thank. Ralph Gilles is the head of design at Fiat Chrysler Automobiles, a guy who can sketch a supercar on a napkin and tell you why cars like the Alfa Romeo 4C make us gooey inside but we instinctively shield our eyes from the Pontiac Aztek. He's also a lifelong tinkerer.

Gilles is building a hot-rodded 1974 Alfa Romeo GTV. His spacious three-car garage, complete with a lift and red-painted floor, is filled with GTV parts. The car's four-cylinder engine block hangs from a stand, its transmission sits on the floor, and folding tables hold the dashboard, the wiring harness, and various other bits. Gilles subbed out the bodywork, but he plans on doing all the mechanical assembly himself.

As a top executive at one of the world's largest companies, frequently shuttling between FCA's U.S. and Italian headquarters, where does he find time for all of this? Is his Alfa a creative outlet separate from his day job, unbound by federal vehicle regulations and production costs? I've known Gilles for a while, so on a quiet Saturday afternoon, I stopped by his home outside Detroit, curious. He was in the middle of putting the Alfa's crankshaft into its block.

"Working on cars is more than just a hobby," he said. "It helps me with my work." Gilles went on to describe what he calls the "cold eye"— a working state where he feels he makes his best decisions. "Monday mornings are an extremely valuable time for me. I come in after a weekend of turning wrenches not thinking about work. That's when my mind is freshest. When I have my cold eye, not influenced by the distractions that pile up during the week."

Previous: 1971
Lamborghini Miura S.
Photo by Steve Cucinotta

Opposite: Fiat
Chrysler head of design
Ralph Gilles assembling
his Alfa engine.
Photo by Sandon Voelker

Gearheads often throw around the phrase "wrenching is life." Over the past decade, this country has seen a growing movement of folks reclaiming home tasks that ordinary people have long farmed out, from raising chickens to brewing beer. Call it a small-scale revolt from our digital lives. In his book *The Revenge of Analog: Real Things and Why They Matter*, David Sax wrote, "Surrounded by digital, we now crave experiences that are more tactile and human-centric." Working on cars, especially the older and more analog, is a perfect example of that.

One of the best writers currently verbalizing the why of tinkering with cars is Boston's Rob Siegel (see page 60). Siegel is an engineer by day but an enthusiastic amateur mechanic by night, and he wrote a terrific book about his garage adventures called *The Hack Mechanic: How Fixing Old BMWs Made Me Whole*. Among my favorite passages, this one sticks out: "I'm centering myself, focusing on one thing, solving a problem, controlling my world." He goes on to explain that modern life contains few opportunities for that kind of restorative experience.

It turns out there's a good reason for all of this and a mental benefit to handwork. "It's called incubation," said Dr. Colleen Seifert, a psychology professor at the University of Michigan. "The idea is to give the mental side of your brain a break and work on a task that's physically driven. The physical task has relatively clear steps to move forward, like a nut goes on the end of a bolt. So you get in the zone where you're moving ahead. It's a sequence of physical activities you do over a period of time. You can think of the work like a distraction, but it's like using other parts of your brain, giving the parts considering a problem a break. And during that phase is when your mind can wander—generate ideas, make connections and associations you haven't thought about in a long time. It's when the best ideas occur."

In other words, it's how you get your cold eye.

We removed shop classes from our schools decades ago, but signs suggest we're coming back around to appreciating the value of manual labor and making things. Generally speaking, the shop-class change took root in the Nineties—a 1996 *New York Times* story headlined "The School Bell Tolls for Shop Class" documented how most high schools removed that kind of teaching in favor of college prep curricula. Let's set aside discussion of whether all kids should go to college and instead consider the life skills taught in those shop classes: the basic safety strategies, how things work, and of course, the self-reliance and satisfaction of being able to tighten a hinge without having to call a carpenter. We're learning that shop can actually help make us better thinkers.

I wouldn't have had the confidence to start tinkering in my garage if it weren't for Mr. Palubniak, the wood-shop teacher in my high school. We called him "Mr. P." I tell my kids that, even though I remember almost nothing of my mid-Eighties high-school experience, I remember his classes. I use his words when I tell anyone coming into the garage to put on safety glasses, and I hear his voice in my head, rising an octave and excited, whenever I'm presented with a vexing problem or mistake. Even though Mr. P. didn't teach auto shop, he passed along a foundation of curiosity and joy in making things that I now cherish.

Mr. P.'s words resonated with me again some 20 years ago, as I struggled to remove a rusted bolt from the rear hub of a 1988 Honda CRX. At the time, I had just wormed my way onto the staff of *Car and Driver*, a dream job I moved across the country to pursue. I was no writer, but the head guy thought my engineering degree would be useful, so after a year of paying my dues by washing cars and fetching lunch, I was hired as a junior editor.

Unfortunately, my presence made life decidedly worse for the managing editor, who had to make my writing suitable for publication. It was admittedly no small task. I had no background in the skill, and he wasn't in the mood to play personal tutor. To make matters worse, I thought I could muscle my way through and turned in truckloads of drafts, each more ham-fisted than the last. They were all sent back with red-pen marks, but also cutting insults written in capital letters, like "WHAT THE F*** IS THIS?" and "THIS IS SO BAD I DON'T KNOW WHERE TO START."

Setting aside his bedside manner, I knew he was right. I also knew that I was learning, and that if I wanted to stick around, I had to improve. But there's no formula for writing, no magic-bullet variable for solving the whole thing. Like so many overconfident 20-somethings, I banged out reams of copy, page after page, certain I could learn anything. The insults hurtled back, cutting deeper and deeper. At night, I retreated to the garage, to a nut that didn't want to leave its axle.

For Mr. P., every problem was an opportunity to try something else. Staring in on that CRX, he would have gleefully said, "Now we get to use the big guns." I methodically brought out longer and longer breaker bars and used a torch to heat the nut. It eventually came loose, a small measure of success that helped blunt what I couldn't achieve at work. I banged my head on the keyboard at *C/D* for years, enduring the continual reminders that I was unfit or perhaps just stupid. I also loosened and tightened a whole lot of nuts. There was never a day when someone came to me and said, "Nice. You got this." The only thing I can say is that I'm somehow still getting paid to write. Looking back, with the knowledge of incubation, would I be here, writing these words, if not for those nights in the garage? I doubt it.

There are signs that shop classes are returning, or at least recognition that they should. Although widespread change has yet to happen, the topic is frequent fodder for news sites and blogs, and a few schools are rolling the dice. High schools in my hometown of Ann Arbor, Michigan, lost shop classes years ago, even though the town is 40 minutes from Detroit and well within the city's cultural orbit. That's why I was surprised, recently, when I saw a flier for a local private school, advertising that it now offered shop.

On a sunny May morning, I walked into the office of Dr. Siân Owen-Cruise. She's the head of the Rudolf Steiner School in Ann Arbor, one of about 160 American schools based on the Waldorf teaching philosophy. The Waldorf method, which dates to 1919, uses a less regimented approach to education. Kids are allowed ample opportunity to nurture their creative side through music and art, and they spend a bunch of time outside being kids. The point is the encouragement of imagination and natural problem solving. Many Waldorf schools eschew computers and technology in the classroom, even the one located in Silicon Valley. That school has gotten a lot of recent press because the majority of its

Tools at rest.
Photo by Amy Shore

Automotive and motorcycle writer Peter Egan in his personal shop.
Photo by Nick Berard

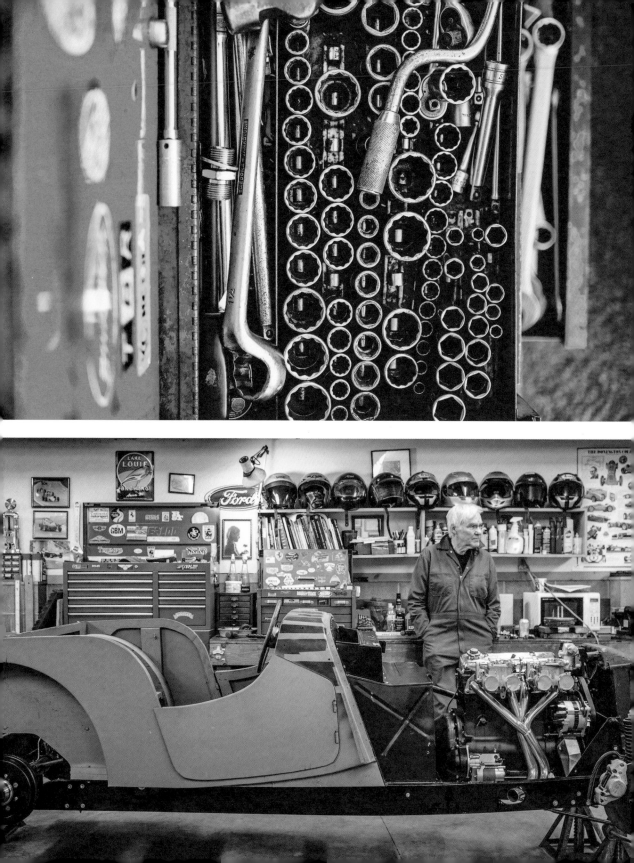

parents work in the technology industry, yet they've chosen to send their kids to a place where tech is limited.

"We believe," Owen-Cruise said, "there's something really good for the soul in making something yourself." But there's a practical side, she noted. Handwork is related to brain development and to "maximizing the capacity of the brain to approach things in new ways." The school's shop class is offered to 10th graders because that's when kids start to drive. The focus isn't rebuilding engines but learning core competencies for life—and opening a door. "We believe there's something not only immediately valuable, developmentally, in those things, but also in the long term to be able to engage in."

Perhaps Waldorf kids will discover, like many of us, that the automobile is a perfect canvas. Any car represents countless hours of ingenuity and creativity, each new example building on the ones before it. They're complex enough to spark interest and curiosity, yet also tangible and tactile. There's a physics lesson in every part.

The Joy of Problem Solving

BY ROB SIEGEL

People come to working on cars through different paths. Some arrive tinkerers, maybe having replaced a shower head or tightened a loose jack in an electric guitar. Others may never have held a wrench. Before I was a car guy, I was a bicycle guy. I was used to looking at something, figuring out how it worked, and fixing it. So 42 years ago, when coolant began streaming out of my just-purchased, three-year-old Triumph GT6, it wasn't too hard to figure out that the thing with the belt on it was the water pump, to see that it was leaking through the seal and bearing, and to ascertain which bolts I needed to undo in order to remove and replace each. The satisfaction was enormous, and I got myself back on the road at low cost. I've been doing it ever since.

It's easy to think the appeal of wrenching is economic, and part of it certainly is. After spending the money to purchase the car of our dreams, many of us don't have much dough left over for hauling the vehicle into a repair shop every time it hiccups. Economics aside, many folks find the process meditative, almost Zen-like. If, in your day job, you deal with the abstract, or punch numbers into a keyboard, coming home to the garage and swaying the fate of a physical object can be an intoxicating contrast.

For me, the problem-solving aspect is downright addictive. Take something as simple as a nonfunctional windshield washer. On most older cars, failure can usually be traced to five things—the fuse, circuit voltage, the motor itself, the washer switch, or a restriction in the fluid line. Once you understand that, you step through the process: Check the fuse. Connect a multimeter to the terminals on the washer motor. If you measure voltage and the motor doesn't turn, it's a bad motor. If there's no voltage, it's probably a bad switch. If the motor turns and fluid doesn't come out, there's probably a restriction in the line or a plugged nozzle. There's not really much else. (Okay, truth be told, I once had a washer motor that turned, but no fluid came out, and the line was clear. When I disassembled the motor, I saw that the little impeller responsible for moving the fluid had fallen off its driveshaft. That was pretty cool. But I fixed it.)

In a world of intractable problems, you can't personally fix healthcare or eliminate bigotry, but you sure as hell can fix your windshield washers. There's a clear beginning and a clear end, and finding that end feels great.

If you don't know how great, well, I strongly recommend you give it a shot. And remember, too, that the tougher problems tend to result in sweeter victories. My '72 BMW Bavaria recently had an intermittent-running issue. Sometimes, the car would struggle to maintain rpm. Other times, it would simply die. I noticed when this problem happened that the tachometer would drop to zero, the needle hitting the "engine off" stop. Since the tach in that car runs off a signal from the ignition coil, this was an indication that the ignition was cutting out. The coil, the spark-plug wires, the cap, and the rotor appeared fine. The problem ended up being a loose screw holding the ignition condenser to the distributor, which prevented the condenser from grounding and thus from operating properly. When I tightened the screw, the problem disappeared. Zero cost, satisfaction off the charts. Or take the time my '73 BMW 2002tii, a mechanically fuel-injected car, developed a vexing stumble above 3000 rpm. I sorted the fuel system stem to stern, swapped every single ignition component with those from another car, and I still couldn't make the problem go away. Finally, out of desperation, I removed the injectors and discovered that one of them contained a broken pintle spring. In the years since, I have yet to meet a single mechanic, whether DIY or professional, who has seen a similar failure. When I replaced the injector, the problem went away. You don't often get *Eureka!* moments like this while fixing cars, but that repair offered a sweetness that I'll bask in for years.

So, fix your own car. Troubleshoot its problems. Sure, you'll save money, but that's not the point. When we fix something, we get to assert some degree of control over a world gone mad. And if you didn't read those last words because you got up and went off to check your condenser screw, well, I don't blame you!

Rob Siegel has been writing the column "The Hack Mechanic" for over 30 years. He is the author of five books and owns nine vintage BMWs and a dead Lotus Europa (the car that proves that men, in fact, can't be taught).

5 / THE PEOPLE YOU MEET

"LISTEN, MAN, IT'S SIMPLE. JUST ASK FOR HELP." And with that, Dan Binks neatly verbalized a maxim we would all do well to heed. Binks is the chief mechanic of Chevrolet's Le Mans–winning Corvette team. He's an expert fabricator, mechanic, and teacher. While interviewing Binks for a magazine story, I asked him about training new mechanics. The greatest hurdle, he said, was teaching people that there's no shame in admitting you need help. "How else do you learn?" he asked.

That admittance is a tall hurdle for many of us. Who wants the boss to know he or she doesn't have the answer? The feeling is understandable, if misguided, in the workplace, but it can be even more counterproductive when it comes to our leisure activities. When we gather around the people who share our passion, the desire to be seen as the expert can be strong. Competence can seem directly related to status. We want to brag about rebuilding the engine ourselves or fixing that spongy brake pedal. Add in shyness, and how the internet can encourage a person's introvert tendencies, and you're a good way toward explaining why a lot of people miss out on what is perhaps the car hobby's richest aspect: engaging with new people.

I've never been afraid to be the idiot in the room. I know what I know, but I don't know what you know, so I try to keep my mouth shut and listen. I can't tell you where this trait came from. Perhaps long ago I got comfortable with my limited mental capabilities and decided just to own them. There are risks, though. Experience has taught me that I tend to be a little too trusting of anyone who sounds like an expert. After 30 years of messing around with cars, I've also learned that the accountant-by-day acquaintance who says he can re-cover my seat probably

Corvette Racing chief
mechanic Dan Binks.
Photo by Andrew Trahan

63

can't. Or at least can't do it better than I could. So when I'm in over my head, I go to the people who make their living working on cars.

But there's a difference between the mechanic who keeps the family minivan on the road and the one you need for your old car. The former has a rich and regimented system of information available for almost any job. A book or web portal will tell him, for example, that replacing a master cylinder on a certain late-model vehicle is a 1.5-hour task. The vintage-car mechanic deals in the unknown. Replacing that master cylinder on your 1950s classic is probably a similar job, but where do you get a replacement? And what if the new one doesn't fit? Once a car gets past a certain age, simple repairs are trips into the unknown. You're going to need services rarely found on Yelp.

For those jobs, you're looking for the oddballs, the mechanical artists you meet by word of mouth who have made their passion their work. If you're lucky, they have room in their schedule and can take on your project. Paying attention to what the experts do has taught me more than I ever expected.

IN 2007, I bought a 1955 Ford Country Squire from a couple in Colorado. This wasn't just any '55 Ford—it was *the* car my father had owned from the time I was born, in 1970, until 1993, when he needed money and sold the wagon.

Dad died in 2002, a few weeks before my first kid was born. I don't remember exactly what made me track down the car. Dad and I were not close, and we rarely spoke. That gnawed at me, though, like I had let him down. I remember feeling as if there were something I needed to put away in order to move on. Finding his old car took a year of paper chasing and phone calls. When I finally got in touch with the people who owned it, I told them my story, and we settled a deal. I shipped the wagon to my home in Michigan, but as I waited for it, another idea formed: I decided to drive the Ford to Rochester, New York, where my dad grew up. And then to my mom's house in New Jersey.

I wanted to learn some of what had shaped my dad. The trip seemed like a good way to visit relatives and friends and fill in the gaps. And if it didn't turn out to be this wonderful, cathartic experience, well, a road trip in an old car didn't seem like a terrible consolation prize.

The previous owners told me the Ford was in perfect shape, ready to go. Because a little insurance never hurts, I wanted to have someone else look at the car. A friend who taught automotive mechanics at the local community college suggested I contact a recent grad named Chance. He called him the sharpest kid who had come through his class and said Chance had yet to find a permanent gig.

Chance told me he was game, so one evening, I drove the Country Squire over to his parents' house a few miles outside of town. Several outbuildings on the property held cars—an old Porsche 928, a dune buggy, a pickup. When I climbed out of the Ford, Chance and his dad, Bill, walked out of the house to meet me. We drove the car into their garage to discuss the next step.

Bill owned a local machine shop, turning out prototype parts and whatever else people asked him to make. He was also a hot rodder, building souped-up machines at night and then selling them to fund his next build. I had come to the right place. Bill didn't volunteer this information, but a bit of gentle asking pulled it out. He deftly made it clear that Chance was in charge of this project.

Their friendship was obvious. As we finished business and kept talking, they told of mutual adventures, screwups, and their favorite cars. It felt a little like the kind of father-and-son relationship you only see in the movies. Months after we met, Chance went to work with his father, opening a small business machining and rebuilding engines in an adjoining room. I found excuses to visit, from welding a bicycle frame to repairing a cracked differential case. Presented with a vexing problem, Chance would say, "I dunno, let's ask the old man." Bill would then come over. Rather than give the answer, he'd ask Chance what he thought. They'd then debate a few things and arrive at a solution. There was never any yelling or tension. They both had confidence in their abilities, but it was wrapped in remarkable humility.

This kind of family dynamic was new to me. I don't wish to drag my childhood through the mud; I was luckier than many other people. But my father always seemed mythical, there but not there. He rarely seemed happy, mostly burdened by the pressure of providing for our family of five. The payoff should have been some bond with his kids. At least with me, that didn't happen.

For a long time, I thought I was at fault. On my Ford trip, however, I learned that I belong to a long line of troubled men. In Rochester, my uncle Jim took me on a tour of the places my family had inhabited. The first was a house where a young Harris Webster, my grandfather, had come home one day to find his father hanging from a rope in the basement. Next came a small bungalow where my father returned from school one afternoon and learned that his father, Harris, had simply gone AWOL. That was in 1948. My dad was six years old. He never heard from his father again.

Something about watching Bill and Chance gave me hope. They were a model, of sorts, for how I wanted to behave with my own kids. After I had gotten to know Bill a bit more, he and I went to dinner one evening. Midway through the meal, I asked about his relationship with Chance. How'd he do it?

I half expected Bill to ask me what I was doing bringing it up—guys gathering to talk cars rarely get into the softer subjects. But he was open. "That's a good question. The fact is, I don't know. I'm grateful for it. I just tried to follow his lead, to be there and willing, but not intrusive." It's a cliché to say there is no user manual for life, no pat answer. But I'd seen what was possible. Bill eventually closed his business and retired. Chance took a job with Chrysler, got married, and had a kid. They're still tight.

THERE IS NO SIGN OUTSIDE Bruce Philip's shop in Ypsilanti, Michigan. I found it in the days before smartphones, thanks to a local car-nut friend. One fall day, I followed those directions down a side road that parallels active train tracks and parked among a cluster of old utilitarian warehouses. Bruce's place felt more like a temple to me than

The car as social network.
*Photos by Amy Shore (top)
and DW Burnett (bottom)*

any of the Catholic churches my mom had once dragged me to. You could tell the warehouse had been around for a while, but it wasn't dirty. Vintage cars, stored here while not in use by their owners, inhabited most of the floor space. Bruce's area took up the south wall, where a bank of windows had been replaced by glass block. Sunlight bathed two bays and a couple of partly disassembled cars. A small, low-ceiling room next to the bay served as Bruce's office and workshop. Fabric racks and tools lined the walls, and a large wooden table dominated the center of the room. The only thing on the table was a sewing machine.

The aroma was intoxicating. Motor oil dominated the air, with hints of leather and perhaps glue. It made the place feel comforting, a home base of knowledge and expertise.

Bruce is a burly man in the second half of his life. He wears a leather apron, a full beard, and reading glasses. We exchanged greetings, and then he walked around my '55 Ford wagon. The foam in the bottom seat cushion had deteriorated over time, so driving the car now felt like sitting on bed springs. Repairing something like this always invites a cascading series of "might as well" repairs or upgrades not critical but cheaper to do when one is already working in the area. In my case, replacing the foam naturally meant replacing the upholstery, too.

However, for me, the Ford's stained and worn seat fabric holds its soul. Every blemish and tear brings back a moving memory of my deceased father. I'd much rather endure the uncomfortable seat than lose the upholstery. For this delicate job, everyone I talked to said I needed Bruce.

Bruce worried that removing the seat fabric, which was brittle with age, would likely destroy it. Consequently, I wasn't sure what to do: Take the risk or leave it. I stood there, stuck in thought. Bruce broke the silence. "Leave it here," he said, "and I'll see what I can do."

Time passed. I didn't need the car for anything specific, so I was patient. Every once in a while, I'd pop into Bruce's shop unannounced. During those visits—some were over in 30 seconds while others were more relaxed—I learned all about the challenges of his restoration business— chief among them, how customers rarely understand the time required to do something right. Bruce wouldn't half-ass to a price point, but old cars are usually someone's hobby vehicle, operated on limited funds. Or people would tell him how the internet said a task could be done in much less time than he quoted. ("Then go have the internet fix it!")

Bruce's past trickled out in these discussions, pieces here and there. He grew up in Detroit in a creative family that liked home crafts. Working alongside his mom and sister, Bruce discovered a passion for sewing, fashion, and leather. He became restless and left Detroit for San Francisco at 16, in 1972, financing the trip by selling leather goods. He bounced between Michigan and San Francisco for a couple of years, slowly growing his leather business. His cars always had his own custom interiors, which were often noticed. Leather work on cars and luggage funded a partying lifestyle, he said, that isn't appropriate to share. "It was the Seventies," he told me.

College didn't work out. Bruce traveled around, taking jobs with anyone he thought might have something to teach. More often than not, he'd leave within a year. By 1982, he had landed in Austin, Texas, and opened a small store and studio. He made leather S&M gear and continued to craft custom car interiors for local celebrities like Jimmie Vaughn. He started a family and had two kids. This prompted stability, and cars paid better than leather, so shortly thereafter, he took a job with White Post Restorations, a large vintage-car shop in Virginia.

If there's one constant in Bruce's life, however, it's that he's a craftsman who wants things done a certain way. Shortly after moving, Bruce left White Post and opened his own shop. He called it Coachtrimmers. His timing could not have been better as the late Eighties saw the first steep climb in classic-car values. Ferrari Daytonas from the early Seventies were suddenly million-dollar cars. Jaguar E-types went from throwaway sports cars trading for a few grand to coveted machines with six-figure price tags. Bruce rode the wave for 20 years, eventually uprooting to return to Michigan. That was in 2010, a few years before I met him.

It took a while, but I eventually pulled my eyes away from Bruce and his work and began to see the finer details of his Ypsilanti workshop. It was fastidiously neat, for one. When I thought he was in the mood,

I'd ask about the tools hanging on the rack. Most were custom-made for stretching fabric or unraveling a seam.

"You can't do this stuff with a Craftsman," he'd joke. Bruce, it turned out, had a healthy sense of humor. Over time we got to know each other, and he was generous with his time, explaining the details of other projects in his shop. I think he enjoyed passing along his knowledge, evidenced by his son apprenticing alongside him.

The Ford was ready after about six months. On the way to pick it up, I prepared myself for the bill. I had not asked about it in advance, assuming that Bruce's talk about "doing things right" was simply setting me up for a whopper. The total came to $1200. The seat was perfect, and Bruce had somehow managed to save the original fabric. No more sitting behind the wheel with springs poking my backside. The driving experience had been transformed.

"That fabric is pretty far gone," Bruce said, "but I knew what it meant to you to keep it."

I did some quick mental math: At, say, $90 per hour, Bruce had charged me for roughly two days of labor. Not a lot, when you consider he had to wrestle with the heavy seat, then carefully remove the fabric and stretch it back in place, saving the whole thing. Oh, he said, and while the car was there, he adjusted the brakes, too.

Two days for all of this? The job would have taken me weeks to do and looked nowhere near as good.

A few years later, I came across a 1969 Porsche 911 that had been sitting in a barn for 30 years. I bought it because I wanted a project; 911s are one of the few widely available cars that will retain enough value after extensive work that you won't lose your shirt paying for time and parts. Plus, this particular car still had its original bits, from the fussy mechanical fuel injection to the rare map pockets in the doors.

Still, the car was in rough shape. I thought I could handle the mechanical work, but there were a couple of rust spots that had to be fixed, and the interior required a complete refresh. I inquired at a couple of body shops. Neither was interested in anything less than a complete body repaint. They were busy commercial operations making

Camaraderie at a vintage-car event.
Photo by Amy Shore

1970 Nissan Skyline 2000GT-R "Hakosuka."
Photo by Matt Tierney

their dough on insurance jobs.

It wasn't the right fit. I needed Bruce.

"What did you get yourself into this time?" he joked.

I expected Bruce to tell me I was a fool. This was years after he had done the Ford's seats, and his shop had grown busier. Bruce now had a full-time mechanic on staff and a handful of customer restoration projects stacked up, awaiting completion. He had turned away friends of mine who went to him, on my recommendation, for small jobs. I could almost hear his words: "Don't waste my time."

But Bruce understood what I was after. He knew I didn't want a perfect paint job, because then I would panic at every stone chip. He knew I liked to play mechanic. He also knew I trusted him and would treat him with respect.

A game plan formed. Bruce immediately rattled off a handful of things I shouldn't even consider tackling, noting that my amateur efforts would be noticed by a buyer if I decided to sell. Those were mostly interior items. New carpet kits rarely fit right, he said, so they would need altering and new edges to mimic original equipment.

A skeptic might argue that Bruce was being self-serving, but what he did next put the kibosh on that notion. The holy grail in the old-car world is a skilled painter and body expert who will take small jobs. Body shops generally fall into two camps: larger, insurance-focused operations, which thrive on volume, and restoration pros who do only whole cars. Both are pricey if you want good work. Getting the stuff in between done right is tricky. References are essential. Bruce, no surprise, had a guy.

"Strip all the stuff off the car," he said, "and I'll call my buddy Sam." Sam then did something unheard of in the world of body guys, much less classic-car wrenches of any flavor: He made a house call.

A battered 1986 Mercedes 300E rolled into my driveway. Sam's 12-year-old son was in the passenger seat. When Sam climbed out, I noticed his hands were large and calloused. He was in his mid-40s. He walked into the garage, saw the Porsche, and announced, "Aw, man, I haven't seen one of these in years!"

We chatted as he looked around. I briefly wondered if Sam would find some fatal flaw on the car that I had missed, an indication that my buying it had been a massive mistake.

"Dang," he said. "This thing is solid. Where did you find it?"

Sam was the opposite of Bruce. No prickly veneer. He was so warm and friendly that I asked him about it. "Oh, I had a struggle with the bottle," he said. "I lost about 10 years to it and spent some time in jail. I've been sober now for 12 years. That experience either changes you for the better, or you die." I tried not to look too thankful that my oldest son was in the garage and heard those words.

Bodywork and painting require someone with a unique personality. Those jobs demand hours of nearly mindless sanding and finishing, plus an artist's touch with a spray gun. "I just get lost in it," Sam told me, "and I love the finished result."

His pride was obvious. His day job, he said, was in a commercial body shop, fixing everyday sedans and trucks. Small jobs for people like me were what he did for fun. "I love cars, and it lets me be a part of the project. I like to see them finished and to help people get them finished."

"This one is going to be tricky," he said, looking at the Porsche. The car wore a decades-old and faded repaint, and matching its hue would be tough. "I'll first have to polish the entire car to see how much color I can bring back and then do my best to match it."

Sam's shop was actually a two-car garage attached to a small suburban home. I didn't ask if the whole affair was legal, but I did think to put a cap on the budget. "No problem," he said. In the following weeks, he voluntarily texted me photos of his progress. "Got it down to metal tonight," one read. Then, "Ready to paint." And then, finally, "Come and get it!" I couldn't tell where Sam's repair ended and the original bodywork began. The final cost was 10 percent under my budget cap, but I gave him the full amount.

Our texting continued. I'd update Sam on my progress with the car, and we'd tell jokes. And then, one day, disaster. While raising the car on the two-post lift in my garage, I stupidly left a door open. It caught on a nearby shelf as the 911 rose. I heard the crunch and immediately put the car back on its wheels. The door no longer shut easily.

Horrified, I called Sam. "I'll be right over."

He looked at it. "Not a big deal. These things sometimes sag." I had merely tweaked the hinges, he said. Then he grabbed the bottom of the door, heaved it up, and tried to shut it. He repeated the process a couple of times until the door once again neatly clicked shut. I didn't know how to thank him. "I just want to see this thing on the road," he said.

And so did Bruce. He actually texted me to ask when I was dropping off those interior pieces. By the end of that summer, I had delivered two large boxes to Bruce: armrests, map pockets, and various interior bits misshapen and faded by time. Few of them seemed salvageable, but I had hoped to reassemble the car over the coming winter and then have Bruce install new carpet the following spring.

As I had with the Country Squire, I stopped by Bruce's shop to hang out and check in. I watched as he reglued edges or heated the plastic— always just enough to make it pliable, never so much that it melted— clamping it into makeshift molds. His work was clearly ad hoc, figuring things out as he went.

About a year after starting the project, I drove the Porsche to Bruce's shop for the new carpet. I was feeling a certain amount of pride in reaching that milestone, so naturally, Bruce had a jab: "I didn't think I'd see this day." We talked for a bit, and I told him about a whistling noise I'd noticed from a door. I suggested he replace the rubber seal, but he scoffed, waving his hand. "Leave it to me."

A couple of weeks later, the carpet was in. Perfectly applied, not a wrinkle. And although the wind whistle was gone, the original seal remained. I looked at him. "How'd you do that?" I asked.

"I have to keep some secrets."

I keep in contact with Bruce and Sam. We run into each other at shows or grab lunch, but I sometimes simply text a photo of my car to one or the other, thanking them for their work. I am, of course, glad to have benefited from their time and knowledge. But the things I'm most grateful for have nothing to do with the car.

A Restorative Process

BY **AARON ROBINSON**

People think the most difficult thing about restoring a Lamborghini Espada is rebuilding its V-12 engine. Well, it isn't. That's just the most expensive part. What caused the most frustration, what reduced me to a puddle of tears and a torrent of cursing, was the power-window mechanism. The Espada—a four-seat, front-engine hatchback that magazines back in the day dubbed "the family Lamborghini" and "a 155-mph Rolls-Royce"—raises its windows electrically using a cable and pulley arrangement in each of the car's doors. Or at least it does that sometimes. I'm fairly certain the mechanism was designed as a weapon by some junior-grade flunky in the North Korean psyops department, intended to bring down the West by fostering madness and suicidal despair. And it nearly worked.

I embarked on the restoration of my first Lamborghini Espada in 1996, shortly after buying the car. That particular Espada was then 27 years old, and I was 27 years old, and one of us was making rash decisions based entirely on youthful confidence. The entirety of my wrenching achievements at the time consisted of a partial restoration of a 1966 MG Midget, a few oil changes on various daily drivers, and one star-crossed attempt to replace the gearbox oil in my 1978 Toyota Corolla using a turkey baster and a pie pan.

In other words, I was not ready for what I found in that seller's garage in Reading, Pennsylvania, in 1996. Nor was I ready for the two other buildings we had to visit to collect all the Espada's disassembled and scattered parts. The stripped block of the Giotto Bizzarrini–designed V-12 had been sitting on the seller's desk for a decade, and cobwebs hung between the main bearings. The crank was in one building, the heads in another. Boxes of aluminum castings and filthy carburetors and bags of nuts and small screws and random springs and unidentifiable rubber and bronze thingies followed me home. My friend Les Jackson, who had mentored me through the rebuild of the MG's engine, declared it would be "an easy two-year restoration." It wasn't.

But I had wanted that car ever since I was 10 years old, when I first saw a picture of an Espada in a book. I can't really explain it, other than to say that I was beguiled by that rakish Marcello Gandini shape and the sheer eccentricity of a 150-mph hatchback four-seater. I've always been drawn to oddballs, and the Espada was king of the weirdos.

I certainly never thought I would own one. I didn't grow up in a car family;

my dad drove a succession of Oldsmobiles. The Espada appeared, not long after I finished my MG, in that gateway drug to all bad decisions, *Hemmings Motor News,* for $10,000. Ten grand! It seemed doable, even though I was at the time making $27,500 a year as the associate editor of a trade magazine for car dealers. I came up with five grand and borrowed the rest from a bank, my dad offering not to loan me the money but to buy a savings bond that I could use as collateral. "I want the business to be between you and the bank, not you and me," he said. I didn't understand it then, but I do now.

Back then I was living in Arlington, Virginia. The Espada went into the garage of our rented house, and all the parts went into the basement. My boss at the time was excited when he heard I had bought an old Lamborghini in pieces. "I got you now!" he said with glee.

With Les's help, I built a poor man's vehicle lift, a three-foot-high cradle made from two-by-six boards, onto which a group of about 15 friends helped lift the gutted body so I could clean and strip it for painting. A year later, after Les and I hurriedly threw the engine together in his garage, I was forced to

Robinson during the early stages of his Lamborghini restoration.

move the whole pile to Michigan behind a rented Ryder truck so my wife, Tina, could start graduate school. I took six months off from the restoration to get our new house and my new career in order and then resumed work. Another two years passed, Tina graduated and went out on the road as a traveling consultant, and I spent most of the four evenings I was alone each week working on the car. I sewed a new headliner. I painted and rebuilt the brake calipers. I spent hours wet-sanding the radiator's twin aluminum fan shrouds, hoping for a chromelike gleam, and then decided they really should be painted black, as original.

Because Espadas were then cheap and unloved, I didn't worry about keeping the car original, so I made burled-walnut inserts for the dash to dress it up a bit. It took weeks to lay down the requisite 10 or 12 coats of polyurethane varnish, wait for it to fully cure, sand most of it off, and then carefully lay down another coat until the varnish was deep enough to swim in. I tried my hand at French-stitching new upholstery, first on the center console. It looked like a six-year-old had scribbled on the material with a Sharpie, so I gave the work to a professional. My Espada, the 113th built out of a 10-year production run of 1217, was a rare Series 1. As such, it had the original bizarre hexagonal dash, a nightmare to upholster. When I went to pick up the interior bits, the trimmer, who in a previous life had sewn concept-car interiors for the auto industry, took my money and said, "Don't ever bring me one of these again."

If the worst part of a restoration is the cleaning and degreasing, the best part, by far, is reassembly. Each day your car looks more and more like it's supposed to. Espadas were handmade, so they go back together by hand—except for the window mechanisms, which require divine intervention. My smartest move was to replace the system's crumbling phenolic pulleys with screen-door wheels running on roller bearings. But reassembly was a living nightmare, one that cannot be described without the use of a diagram and unprintable language. I'd kill to know how the factory did the job, but Lamborghini barely kept records of anything. My procedure, developed over hours of screaming, used a network of zip ties that were carefully cut in sequence so the tension on the lift cable would never relax to the point where it fell off the pulleys.

About that V-12: It's best to think of it as a 3.9-liter motorcycle engine. Compact, complex, artful. Four cams, 24 valves, an aluminum block and head, and most of its power around the 7500-rpm redline. You could write a whole book about how to rebuild this wonderful device, but highlights include castings so soft and porous that studs pull if you look at them funny and oil that weeps straight out the sides of the heads and block. Ceramic coatings now exist to stop the latter, but back then they didn't exist or I didn't know about them. Indeed, back then, before the internet changed everything, if you had questions, you called the guy in Florida who ran the Lamborghini club, and he gave you a few phone numbers to try, and you hoped one of those was for a guy who did his own work and had experienced your particular problem. Ah, the old days!

I was seven years into the project before I first drove the car. The hood was off, there was no side or rear glass, and I was sitting on a milk crate. For years I had been having recurring dreams about the day, and always it was the same: As I drove along, parts fell off the car. Before that point, I had only driven an Espada for about five minutes, and it obviously wasn't this one. That first drive in my own Espada was cut short by explosive backfires, the result of bad ignition condensers. The second drive, months later, was better.

Robinson's Espada, before fresh paint.

One of the 12 unsecured intake trumpets rattled out of one of the six Weber 40 DCOE carburetors and went bouncing down the road. Amazingly, it was undamaged, but I learned not to be lazy and just throw the trumpets on without including the 24 small nuts that hold them in place.

The car eventually reached a decent state of reliability, but it never ran perfectly. It wasn't until years later, after I bought my second Espada, that I learned everything I had done wrong. I moved to California in 2004, and by 2006, I was sick of the Espada and considered selling it. I put a small note on the windshield at that year's Concorso Italiano at Pebble Beach, and sure enough, a guy called shortly thereafter. "I've never seen one of these before in my life," he said. "Tell me about it." A deal was done—an embarrassingly low amount considering how much I had into the car and what they go for now—and Lamborghini Espadas exited my life. Briefly. I bought another in 2011, the 263rd car built, a two-owner Series 2 that still had its original pale green paint and blue leather interior. Like lead, the Espada gets into your bloodstream.

Restoring a car makes you intimate with it like no other experience can, and you lose all fear. When stuff breaks, you just fix it. Heck, you've done it before. An Espada at 80 mph is pulling 4000 rpm. So many moving parts! Do I worry about them? Not really, because I've held each one of those parts in my hand, and I know where to find them if they break.

Which leads to the best reason to restore a car, and the reason why every car enthusiast should try it at least once: Besides learning a ton about cars in general, you gain immense confidence in your own abilities. So many times in that restoration I came up against problems I thought would never be solved. I thought, this is it, I'm just going to push the car into the street and let the city snowplow take it away. But after a while, you begin to believe there is no problem you can't solve. Years later, I still encounter problems elsewhere in life and think, "I bolted together a Lamborghini engine. I took a pile of useless parts in boxes and made it make lovely noises. How hard can *this* be?"

When you restore a car, you save it from the junkyard. But the car also saves you.

Aaron Robinson has written about the car industry for 25 years at Car and Driver *magazine as well as several trade publications. A Michigan native, he has owned everything from a 1938 Buick to a Suzuki Every JoyPop Turbo.*

6/FAMILY HOUR

I KICKED THE KART OVER with a fury that sent tools and spare parts pinging across the shop. Oh, please, I pleaded to the gods of cathartic rage: Purge my frustration. Then my two sons, wide-eyed and summoned by the unfamiliar racket, burst through the garage door.

A wave of shame and regret washed over me. Taking a moment to inhale, I looked down at my hands, slimy with RTV sealant, and tried to recover.

"I lost my cool," I said, forcing a smile. The boys looked a little afraid. Two months ago, in my garage, we had all begun work on a 1969 Chevrolet. This anger was not one of the lessons I had hoped to pass on.

Back then, the car ran fine. My son Sam, who is nine, likes cars almost as much as his old man. He suggested we take our '69 Chevelle wagon to a local drag strip to see what it could do. His 15-year-old brother, John, doesn't share our passion but was curious enough to go along. At the strip, the Chevy scooted down the quarter in 15.02 seconds. Not bad, I thought, for a family hauler nearly a half-century old.

Sam, however, is hooked on a YouTube show called *Roadkill*. It features two buddies resurrecting and modifying junker cars for speed and adventure. At press time, it had almost six million subscribers and more than 37 million views. Sam scoffed at our 15 seconds. "It should be in the thirteens," he announced. "Let's put a Hemi in it."

Never mind the heresy of installing a Chrysler engine in a Chevy, I knew what Sam was saying: He wanted a *Roadkill* experience. How could I say no?

I should back up here. I've never pushed my car hobby on my kids, in part because that doesn't work. No matter how many flea markets my

Webster, his sons, and their 1969 Chevrolet Chevelle.
Photo by James Lipman

81

mom dragged me to in my youth, browsing through piles of junk with her was nothing short of torture. We're all wired with certain tendencies. Some kids follow their parents, some don't. Yet I wondered what we, as a family, were going to talk about at holiday dinners in the future. What stories would be retold? What would our kids remember? It probably wouldn't be the hours my wife and I spend schlepping our three kids to various activities. We needed to find something to do with more impact than watching a movie together.

You go with what you know, so I've tried to create an open-door policy with my car hobby. I make it known what I'm doing in the garage, or why I'm buying or selling one of the revolving-door used cars that grace our driveway. I always invite my kids along for car shows and races, and I try to hide my disappointment when they don't join me. In a family of five—we have a 13-year-old daughter, Abby—it's tricky, if impossible, to find something that pleases everyone. Somebody's always going to suffer, so I'd occasionally shoot for the moon, dragging everyone to a local car race. Nothing stuck.

Like grown-ups do, kids have countless options for their free time. And they're kids, of course, with ever-changing interests. But perhaps Sam's desire with the Chevelle could be the spark to draw the others in. (And if not, I thought, well, the kid had a point: Faster is always better.) It helped that I know plenty of families who do the car thing as a group. My friend James is an automotive engineer. We met while racing in amateur weekend events. The first few times we hung out, I'd marvel at the bloodline army that accompanied him. Wife, kids, brother, mom, dad—all seemingly happy to pitch in. What he pulled off always felt like a mystery. What did they know that I didn't? So I called and asked.

"It's my family's culture," James said. "We all support one another, no matter what, by attending football games, dance recitals, whatever. Racing is simply my turn. I've found that it helps to make them part of it, to give them a job, so they're part of the team, not just watching."

It made sense. In the car industry, several famous family businesses have been successfully passed on through generations. One of my favorite stories is that of the Justice family. After World War II, racing enthusiasts Ed and Zeke Justice started the Justice Brothers oil additive company, which they promoted by sponsoring racing drivers. Their company became part of the motorsports fabric, which meant regular attendance at events like the Indianapolis 500 and the 24 Hours of Daytona. Ed's son, Ed Justice, Jr., went along, living the nomadic racing lifestyle and learning the ropes. Junior eventually took over the company with no less automotive passion than his forebears. Now, decades into his reign, he employs the next generation: his two daughters, Courtney and Caitlyn.

For the Justice family, cars and racing were all they knew. "I started as the company photographer," Junior told me. "Since I was at the races anyway, why not shoot?" He told me his daughters had the same experience as he did. Going to the races at an early age, they were bound to soak it in. "I think as a family we really respect our history. It's a torch that's passed down with an awful lot of passion. For us, it's a bonding thing."

A couple of years ago, as I stood outside a California shop waiting to pick up a motorcycle, I struck up a conversation with a guy standing near his Ford Explorer. He was also waiting, albeit for his daughter, who had agreed to help him replace the Ford's brakes. Sure, he could have managed it by himself at home, but he said he liked to do the job with her, as they'd done when she was growing up. Plus, he mentioned, she had long surpassed his skills, opening a car-repair business that had a very handy lift.

With the Chevelle, I wondered if I was the roadblock. Perhaps my flea-market experience didn't teach me what I needed to know.

I let Sam's idea cool for a while to see if it would fade. But that kid is relentless. He kept talking *Roadkill*. I floated a plan: What if we kept the Chevelle's big-block V-8 and modified it with high-performance parts? "No Hemi?" Sam asked. No, I replied, it's just too expensive. And probably beyond my self-taught mechanical skills.

"Then can we put headers on?"

"Of course. And aluminum heads, too."

Sam was all in. He came up with a name, since every *Roadkill* car has one: Project 13s. We ordered $2700 worth of engine parts and rolled

the car into my garage as winter descended. And that was when the unexpected happened: John began asking if we needed help. I didn't pick up on his invitation at first, because I didn't want him out there if he felt obligated. My wife, however, recognized that he simply liked feeling needed. Clued in, I began asking for him to join me and Sam.

Our old Chevy is relatively simple and not worth much, which made it a perfect canvas. The boys could fumble around with little risk. Sam had to sit on the fenders to work a socket wrench to remove the valve-cover bolts. When he stopped using his second hand to keep the wrench on the bolt, I knew the tool slipping off was a far more effective teacher than me reminding him, for the 800th time, to use two hands. If he dented the bodywork, so be it.

John proved capable, but behind his teenage bravado, he lacked confidence. He'd ask how to do things I knew he could handle. I finally began to give those questions a pat response. "Why would I," I'd say, with as much drama as I could muster, "as a father who loves his son, deprive you of all the things you could learn by figuring it out yourself?" It would usually bring a wry smile.

If there was one thing missing in this tableau, it was the boys' sister, Abby. She didn't want to be left out, but the grease and the mess were, as she put it, "gross." Still, I wanted her around. She liked to paint, so we set up a table and easel in the garage, which let her work while we wrenched. I'd pull her in when there was something fun to do, like buzz off wheel nuts with an impact wrench. At least, I thought, she would know what a wrench does and perhaps get more interested. It seemed to work. She was a part of the team.

We were engaged in what the writer Nicholas Hayes calls "chosen time," an activity that fosters healthy personal interactions. In his book *Saving Sailing,* Hayes convincingly laid out the differences between chosen time and what he calls "chartered time."

"The epitome of the charter," he wrote, "is a visit to a theme park." He argued that a theme park is a carefully orchestrated, shrink-wrapped experience, much like watching a movie. "The charter isn't all bad," he wrote, "it's just not ours." The chosen experience is often messier, but

1969 Chevrolet Chevelle.
Photo by James Lipman

Kris Clewell teaching his daughter how to remove a wheel.
Photo by Kris Clewell

Hayes noted that it tends to hold opportunity for a much richer outcome. "If a choice delivers a positive experience," he wrote, "it becomes a source of personal pride and personal and community growth."

I happen to agree with him. My challenge was thus to make sure our little project didn't bog down. There were great unknowns in what we were doing: How long would this take? Would we finish? Would the car be faster? And holy hell, why don't these headers fit? I also knew a fuse had been lit. If the kids didn't see regular progress, they would lose interest. And so began a great tug of war between progress and letting the kids do the work. Sam doesn't yet have the strength to remove cylinder-head bolts. John is a typical teenage boy, with a millisecond attention span. Abby, well, she's happy painting, but I was concerned about finding places for her to chip in.

The only thing I knew for sure was that the car had to be running by spring. If it sat unfinished by then, I had the feeling it would represent a failure every time one of us went into the garage. That was not a lesson I intended to teach.

THIS IS A LONG WAY OF EXPLAINING how I came to kick over that tool cart. By late January, Project 13s had stalled. The excitement of disassembly had given way to the reality that working on engines, even relatively simple vintage ones, is not what my wife jokingly calls "adult Lego." Bolts can be hard to access. Old gaskets take sweat and elbow grease to scrape off. And even parts marketed as "bolt on" often simply don't fit. Take our new aftermarket headers—a portion of the exhaust system that took hours of hammering to make fit in the engine bay. After that hammering, checking to see if the headers fit in the car meant removing the 40-pound cylinder head. We did this countless times. The big trouble was that the team leader, me, had never rebuilt an engine. Why, again, did I think this was a good idea?

To make sure the kids saw steady progress, I'd keep working after they went to bed, stealing an hour here or there to tackle jobs of which I suspected only I was capable. So that Saturday, I went into the garage by myself to wrestle with the oil-pan gasket. The oil pan is a bowl that bolts to the bottom of the engine. It catches the engine's oil and feeds it to a pump that circulates it back through the engine. Oil pans are usually sealed by a paper gasket. To install a new camshaft and free up a few horsepower, we had to remove a plate that bolts to the front of the engine and also to the pan. Then the whole thing would go back together with a new gasket.

Simple, right? In hindsight, there are a few things I could have done to make the job a lot easier. Suffice it to say that, on that Saturday, I was trying to install the plate and a new gasket. It all fit into a space in the car that wasn't much larger than a shoe box. Then there was the pressure of finishing the work so the kids and I could move on. Every time I'd wedge the gasket in place, it would slip out. I was running out of time. The pressure built up until the innocent little tool cart became lightning's ground. Boom.

Later, at dinner, we all made a joke of my tantrum—a state of frustration the kids were used to seeing in their peers, but not me. When my wife and I were alone together, she wondered if I had gotten in over my head. Should I call in some help? I wasn't proud of the outburst, but I had no interest in bailing out. I rarely lose it, and the kids saw my being human. The real lesson, I said, was in what we did next. Step one was to take a break.

During my previous discussion with Dr. Seifert, the University of Michigan psychology professor, I asked about projects large enough to be worked on by multiple people. "There's something about those paths where you're completing a series," she said, "something about a shared task that really builds relationships." She went on to explain that collective building is essentially the key to all human success. Project 13s was our version of Amish barn raising. More important, she said, there were even more benefits in something called embodied cognition—the notion that our thinking is rooted in the physical world.

"All of our higher cognitive processes are built on our first physical experiences," she explained. "By enacting the physical, you're reengineering or priming the concepts that we first learned. It's truly psychologically compelling to act in the physical world." Project 13s was therefore accomplishing two things: a shared challenge building toward a goal, and engaging my kids in something other than a video game to help them learn more effectively. That was all the nudge I needed.

I realized, too, that I was learning. I had learned to recognize, in my kids and myself, when frustration was overcoming the ability to complete a task. We'd step back and hang around the toolbox, joking about a particularly onerous task, like the drudgery of running a thread cleaner down each of the car's numerous cylinder-head bolt holes. There was a mock celebration when I finally got that oil-pan gasket seated.

We moved on, one little success at a time. Finally, a month after the tool-cart incident, we opened the garage door, letting in the cold winter air. The time had come to start the engine. Or at least turn the key and hope it fired. With plugs stuffed in our ears to shield against the unmuffled exhaust, and John and Sam each holding fire extinguishers, I turned the key.

The moment will stick in my head for a long time: the two of them looking at each other, their exhales visible in the cold, their faces dusted with anticipation and a little bit of worry. God, please start, I thought, at least a rumble. The boys jumped back as the big-block lit off and bellowed, the garage filling with smoke as the engine burned off solvents and assembly lube. I jumped out and we hugged in the racket, saying things to one another no one could hear.

In the following weeks, as we tinkered with the car's timing and idle speed, neighborhood kids tended to wander over, drawn by the noise. There was my John, the insecure teenager with grease on his hands, explaining to the others what we had done. I gave rides, kids piled into the car, rattling the neighbors' windows as we circled the hood.

WE HAVEN'T YET FOUND THE TIME to take the Chevelle back to the drag strip. We will, if for no other reason than Sam won't let us forget. I've tried to keep our garage sessions going, with middling success. I passed my old daily driver, a 1998 BMW 328i, to John; it's his first car, with the provision that old German cars need things and he has to help me keep it going. Abby sometimes paints while we're working, and Sam buzzes in and out. He's still true to form—if a car can't do a burnout, he's not interested.

I wonder, sometimes, what comes next. We might not find another car that engages us like the Chevelle. As a project, an automobile is tough to replace. Its physical size and complexity allow multiple people to take on multiple jobs simultaneously, yet it's compact enough that everyone stays in the same room. On top of that, the Chevelle is a woolly, compelling machine, spitting fire and noise. It seems to carry a kind of latent mystery for the kids—different enough from modern cars that it seems foreign, but new enough that it distantly resembles the cars driven by their parents. My kids probably find it a little familiar, even if they don't realize it.

But that's parenting, I guess. Answers are rarely obvious, so you just do the best with what you have and try to nudge the process in the right direction every so often. If that nudging happens to go down with a V-8 and some Detroit sheetmetal, well, all the better.

We were engaged in "chosen time," an activity that fosters healthy personal interactions. The chosen experience is often messy but holds opportunity for a much richer outcome.

1965 Ford Mustang. *Photo by Andrew Trahan*

PART THREE | BY JACK BARUTH

The Joy of Driving

AS ANIMALS GO, HUMANS MOVE PRETTY SLOWLY.
BUT WE'RE WIRED FOR SPEED.

7 / DESIGNED FOR MASTERY, DRIVEN BY SENTIMENT, WIRED FOR SPEED

SUPERSPEEDWAY. SUPERCHARGED. Superhighway. Super Snake, Super Sport, Super Beetle. Supernatural, then Supernormal.

Our ancestors were surrounded by the supernatural. The sun was a god and the earth was a mother. Every crash of thunder, each rise of the Nile, came from above, or maybe below. Lacking a way to reach the distant and presumably indifferent ears on Mount Olympus and elsewhere, our forebears pumped up the volume: massed chanting, vestal virgins, towers of Babel, human sacrifice at the apex of a slave-built ziggurat.

We don't do quite as much business with the supernatural these days. Instead, we're surrounded by the *supernormal*. Refined sugar and its diabolical cousin, high-fructose corn syrup, targeting with deadly accuracy a class of cells on your tongue that evolved to help you find the fruit with the highest available energy content. Pop music, assembled bit by digital bit in a studio, designed with inhuman precision to stir emotions and responses in a manner both predictable and marketable. The internet, assaulting your caveman mind with a 24/7 light and sound show that promises something better around the corner but always just out of reach.

Last but not least, the vehicle in your driveway. Like those other amusements, it is designed to provide what psychologists call "supernormal stimuli." Human beings have evolved to respond to certain inputs: cold, heat, taste, smell, sound, the sensation of motion generated by our inner ears. We survived thousands of generations by following those stimuli wherever they led—eating sweet things, listening for the ancient rhythms of tribal communication, seeking comfort where it was available. It all worked quite well until the introduction of supernormal stimuli, made by man to appeal to his own deepest instincts and rarely bound by any kind of reason or even common sense. *Did you enjoy eating an apple? Then you'll really like cotton candy.*

It's easy to understand the root evolutionary appeal of many supernormal stimuli, from the ice cream in your freezer to the "after dark" shows available via cable television. The automobile, and the enjoyment thereof, is a slightly tougher nut to crack. It is a compound experience of speed and mastery, enjoyed in many different forms—from leisurely Sunday back-road drives to Formula 1 qualifying sessions. There is no scientific consensus on why driving can be so pleasurable. Yet there is an obvious and unbroken thread that stretches from the unrecorded dawn of prehistory to the precise moment when you open up the throttle on your first sports car or motorcycle.

Start with this: We have always wanted to go faster. In earlier days, speed kept us alive, kept food in our bellies. Our distant ancestors in Africa simply ran the local game into the ground, pursuing antelope and the like on foot for miles upon miles until the animals tired and could be killed. The earliest athletic contests on record contained a diversity of events where speed over time was crucial.

As toolmaking creatures, humans logically created tools for speed over time. The snow ski is perhaps 10,000 years old; the sled is older than that. We have no way of knowing if they were raced, although there is some evidence that skiing was pursued for pleasure in addition to its practical aspects. We know for certain that the chariot race arrived at approximately the same time as the chariot itself and persisted as a means of entertainment long after the military use of such vehicles disappeared.

The lightweight horse-drawn carriage was tremendously popular in Europe from the Iron Age forward, likely because it was fast and relatively affordable. It was frequently used for mere amusement; the phrase "drive in the country" was coined for carriages and made sexy by the fast-moving post chaises that used four horses to pull two passengers. The British lexicographer Samuel Johnson told his biographer, James Boswell, that, "if I had no duties, and no reference to futurity, I would spend my life in driving briskly in a post chaise with a pretty woman."

From the moment the automobile appeared on the scene, it was both feared and lionized for its potential velocity. More than that, it presaged a world where speed and wealth would be directly connected. The aristocracy had always had fancy coaches, but the internal-combustion engine made velocity the new luxury. Available in spades to the buyers of supercharged Mercedes-Benzes or Duesenbergs, and doled out in small doses to the person who traded a Model T for a Model A. Not until the flathead Ford V-8 appeared was there a hint of democracy to the arrangement. Then it was possible for everyone to go as fast as the law allowed, or faster.

Every modern car, therefore, is a supernormal stimulus. Even a Prius can comfortably triple the highest speed of which Secretariat was capable. Yet it's not enough to just go fast; nobody finds it particularly thrilling to ride in the middle seat of a Boeing 737. There has to be more to it than that—and there is.

We enjoy speed more when we confront it head-on. A motorcycle feels faster than a convertible with the top down, which in turn feels faster than the double-paned glass isolation of a luxury sedan. Our sensation of speed is significantly lessened by distance from the ground, which is why drivers of SUVs and pickup trucks are often less able to judge appropriate velocity for conditions. Louder cars feel faster, as do cars with larger windshields. On an autobahn, 120 mph in a Mercedes S-class seems more or less sane, but 40 mph on a scooter filtering through lanes in a Manhattan rush hour gives you a remarkably good idea of how a chariot racer in the Colosseum of Rome must have felt.

These experiences are all available to passengers as well as drivers. So why drive at all? Where's the pleasure in it? That comes from the other half of the equation, which is mastery. Our human reverence for, and enjoyment of, mastery is as old as our love of speed. If not older. Feats of skill and mastery, often involving weapons, are at the heart of our oldest legends. Robert Fitzgerald's translation of Homer's *Odyssey* starts thus:

**Sing in me, Muse, and through me tell the story /
of that man skilled in all ways of contending.**

Those "ways of contending" are tactical and strategic, but they are also athletic and precise. The story's climax happens when Ulysses proves himself to be capable of something none of his rivals can accomplish: shooting an arrow through 12 ax heads in a row. It's a metaphor as much as a story. To master a difficult task, particularly one involving bravery or strength, is the height of felicity in worlds ancient and modern. Our modern Ulysses might be Michael Schumacher, whose skill in all ways of contending enabled him to rebuild Ferrari's Formula 1 team from scratch and then lead it through five championships. Not only was he a brilliant driver, but he had also mastered all necessary aspects of the sport, from selecting talented crew members to knowing when the time was right to press an attack on a temporarily weakened rival.

The modern video game is a perfected supernormal stimulus, offering challenge and reward in precisely measured amounts via an environment under the control of the game's developer. Today's racing games are so good, and so faithful to reality, that there is a growing population of real-world racing drivers who earned their early "wins" behind a screen instead of a windshield. There is still a discernible difference, however, between cyberspace and the world outside, and there remains a tangible difference between the sterile pleasure of winning a video game and the all-encompassing joy of driving a good car fast on a challenging road.

This is where speed and mastery come together. You are traveling at a rate that was effectively impossible for any human being even a century ago, which is thrilling in itself. You are connected to the sights, sounds, and sensations of the road, assaulting your senses in a manner that is undeniably real. Finally, you are exhibiting mastery of the automobile itself, controlling it through your direct physical commands and observing the results of those commands. How could this be anything but thrilling?

But there's more. The act of driving a car at speed is an unmistakable

1962 Ford Thunderbird.
Photo by Sandon Voelker

1978 Pontiac
Firebird Trans Am.
Photo by DW Burnett

declaration of individuality and independence. Walk out to your car, keys in hand. Open the door, and take a seat. What happens next is not the product of a train timetable, a bus schedule, an airplane itinerary. It is entirely up to you. The car can take you from the main street of a heartland American town to the Strait of Magellan or the eternal daylight of Alaska. Each intersection presents four choices, and no permission is needed to choose any of them. You can hammer relentlessly between fuel stops, or you can take every side road that intrigues you. The person on a train is mere cargo, sentient in dribs and drabs; the driver of a privately owned automobile is the captain of his or her ship. Most of us never use our cars for anything but round-trips to work, school, weekend destinations—but it's nice to consider that the car can also be a one-way proposition. From *Rabbit, Run* to *Easy Rider* to *Thelma and Louise,* the automobile has always held the promise of escape.

You got a fast car / I want a ticket to anywhere.

—"FAST CAR," TRACY CHAPMAN

So, naturally, we buy cars that promise the romance of remote destinations: *Tucson, Malibu, Monte Carlo.* Trucks, too, contain the promise of a frontier: *Silverado, Prospector, Sonoma.* We treat our cars like family, give them pet names, occasionally go without so they can have what we think they need or want. We festoon them with stickers, change them to reflect our desires. With each modification and each upgrade we come closer to the Platonic ideal of a car that announces our individuality and augments our own selves.

Then there's the minor matter of automobile as mating call. Sixty years ago, drive-in restaurants and cruising spots vibrated with the energy of V-8 engines and glasspack mufflers. Today, they boom and rumble from impractically powerful and complicated sound systems. The vibe is the same, and it bears a direct kinship with the message sent by the peacock's colorful tail.

Without mastery, without the ability to steer the car in the direction of your every whim, you're just a passenger. Maybe that's why autonomous vehicles feel to us like the sworn enemy of every single human sentiment and emotion described above. It takes the Zen moment at the start of a drive, where all destinations are possible, and replaces it with a cyber-plotted itinerary. It exchanges the noble elements of mastery for a lesser alloy of possession and detachment, turns the illicit thrill of speed into the heartless arithmetic of distance and time. The lovingly customized personal vehicle will give way to the linoleum subway chic of shared operation, easy to wipe clean and frequently in need of said cleaning, because few things in this world are treated worse than a public conveyance. Those quantum collisions of romantic entanglement that occur when a girl in a flatbed Ford swings past a corner in Winslow, Arizona? Gone, replaced by frantic and unpleasant coupling behind curtains and between waypoints on Google Maps.

Nobody ever wrote a love song about a subway.

Nobody has ever felt a deep, personal connection with a city bus.

As above, so below.

Thankfully, we're not there just yet. The automobile is still here for us, with its improbable combination of danger and attraction. It can take you where you want to go, as fast as you can get away with, as skillfully as you can manage. Bring what you want, bring what will fit, bring the people who matter.

Or you can go nowhere at all. You can restore a car to concours perfection, or you can buy a brand-new Corvette and engage in a 10-step process to "correct" the paint and seal it beneath a half-dozen layers of hand-polished wax. Then you can drive it a short distance on the most perfect days before placing it beneath a soft wool cover in the garage. The choice is yours. Best of all, you can always change your mind, fire up that Vette in the season of hot blood, and drive it to Atlantic City or

Las Vegas without so much as a by-your-leave. Even a car that never moves has a certain implied, spring-coiled readiness for action, the way a house cat sleeping on a pillow could choose at any moment to imitate the tiger. No computer-controlled plastic box chained to invisible rails of software and legislation will ever have that potential. Once freedom is surrendered, it does not return without an effort ranging from merely mighty to completely impossible.

I think back to 1979 when my father brought home a brand-new, lemon-yellow MG Midget from the British Leyland dealership near Columbia, Maryland. I'm not sure a more feckless example of a sports car has ever existed. It was a two-decade-old design festooned with hideous "federal" bumpers, raised up on wobbly suspension extenders to meet a new raft of safety regulations, powered by a minuscule engine strangled by incompetently designed emissions-control devices. The dashboard was thickly padded with cheap vinyl. The transmission had a quartet of forward gears, selected not without difficulty through the agency of a long, floppy wand with a crooked knob on top. Time and again, it failed to start for no obvious reason, or it stranded Dad in situations ranging from the humorous (the next street over) to the hazardous (the Capital Beltway). Some months the odometer didn't turn a single digit. After two years, it had four thousand miles on the clock. My father regarded the yellow MG, quite rightly, as both disappointment and failure.

At the age of nine, I comprehended little of this. All I knew was that the Midget had, at its core, a different raison d'être from the sleepy sedans and wobbling wagons that formed the stegosaurian landscape of my youth. It was meant to be driven, not as a means to an end, but for its own sake. Dad's LeSabre was faster, Mom's Cutlass had more style. The Midget had something else.

So I would wait until everyone in the house was asleep, then I would sneak downstairs, open the back door with a practiced hand, and slink into the garage, where the Midget sat alone. I knew the top would be down and the doors would be unlocked, but to operate the latches would invite the chance of discovery. Softly, quietly, I climbed over the driver's

1972 Porsche 911T.
Photo by Kris Clewell

door, my pajamas catching on various protrusions and quality defects. Then I arranged myself behind the absurd molded-plastic wheel.

I imagined the day when I would be able to start the Midget and take it anywhere I wanted to go. I dreamed of winding back roads that led nowhere in particular, the eight-lane concrete ribbons between my home and New York, an arrow-straight desert highway to the romance and adventure of the West Coast. The Midget promised all those things and more. I didn't notice British Leyland's amateurish attempts to make the car even remotely fit for the showrooms of 1979, nor did I care about the fact that certain parts of the car were starting to bubble with rust despite virtually zero exposure to the elements. All I knew was that this car was designed to go somewhere besides the grocery. That was enough.

In the nearly 40 years since, I've gone everywhere I'd hoped the Midget would take me, and some places besides that were too raw and vibrant for a child's imagination. Coastal roads, mountain passes, Appalachian forests, Alabama getaways. I've crossed finish lines in first place, and I've lost races in the first turn. I've crossed the border of all 48 contiguous states while behind the wheel, and I've driven in places where I didn't know enough of the local language to decipher the simplest road sign. There are trips I'd like to forget and ones I would shed blood to experience again.

What I remember most are those precious times I fired up my car with no particular place to go and no precise timetable, owing my punctuality to no one and my presence only to myself. The times when the automobile was my only counselor and echo chamber. The kind of journey that no autonomous vehicle could take, because how could a robot car know where to take you when you don't know yourself? It's not a trip you could explain after the fact to a computer, or a judge, or an accountant. It makes no sense, but it's far from senseless. We need automobiles, even if we can't quite tell you why. Blame it on the supernatural, or credit it to the supernormal. More than a century after the start of the automotive party, the experience remains superb.

What I remember most are those precious times I fired up my car with no particular place to go and no precise timetable, owing my punctuality to no one and my presence only to myself.

1990 Ferrari F40. *Photo by Andrew Trahan*

8 / THE ROAD GOES ON FOREVER

NEVER MIND THE TRACK. *The track is for punks. We are Road People. We are Café Racers.*

—"SONG OF THE SAUSAGE CREATURE," *CYCLE WORLD,* HUNTER S. THOMPSON

What makes a great driving road? Is it the scenery? The condition of the tarmac? The radius of the curves? The lack of constant law enforcement? We have more than four million miles of paved road in the United States, but few of those miles are anything but utilitarian. Some of those few are broadly known and celebrity approved, like Topanga Canyon Road outside Los Angeles. Others, like the triangle of roads in southeastern Ohio used by a few auto magazines for their annual evaluations, are famous within small circles.

If you look hard enough, however, chances are you'll eventually find an escape road of your own. Most enthusiasts develop a sixth sense for them. We spread county-level maps out on tables and look for the most "fractalesque" route from Point Nowhere to Point Somewhere Else. We catch a glimpse of a twisted stretch off the freeway and resolve to backtrack until we find it. We drive every road in a 20-mile radius around our homes looking for that one perfect combination of corners that will make the next grocery-store trip or morning commute a little more exciting.

Then we keep that secret close to us, as if we'd discovered a service entrance to the tomb of Tutankhamen. It's ridiculous, because there is nothing quite so well-known and unmysterious as a road. It was built by dozens or hundreds of people and has since been maintained by a local government. Chances are there's a school bus traversing your own

2017 Bugatti Chiron.
Photo by Richard Pardon

private Nürburgring every morning and afternoon. It doesn't matter. We're dealing with a second level of meaning here. To the tone-deaf, there is no difference between Beethoven and Muzak. Hoi polloi might cover a particular road every day of their lives and understand nothing about it. If Michelangelo were the only one who saw David in the marble, then we might be the only ones who see Eau Rouge in the sharp climb between two Amish farmhouses.

There was once a lot more of that marble buried in the open spaces between America's cities, thanks to a counterintuitive but amusing fact: Building an exciting road is *easier*. The earliest pavement in this country faithfully followed the worn cart paths and Native American trails laid out hundreds of years before; those, in turn, were entirely a function of the variegated East Coast terrain over which they ranged.

All those things we prize in a road—the tight sweep around a blind corner, the vertiginous drop along a hillside that terminates in a short hairpin before resuming its descent, the one-two punch of a left- then right-hander that rocks the car from bump stop to bump stop while the driver heroically saws at the wheel—all the things that, collectively, can be characterized as variety—those are generated, almost automatically, by the terrain of the Smokies and the Cascades and the Sierra and a countless number of folds in the underlying rock.

Until recently, roads were made by laborers with picks, shovels, and a surprising shortage of machinery. Their work followed the path of least resistance on the terrain, which was often thrilling. Ironic, too, because in the era before internal combustion, every one of those blind turns and each vertical foot of grade exacted a real cost in exhausted animals, road accidents, and delayed commerce.

The ur-example of this is probably the Cumberland Road of 1806. It headed west toward the Ohio River at Thomas Jefferson's nearly imperial command, soon acquiring the sobriquet of the National Pike. The innovation of a compacted-gravel surface allowed Conestoga wagons to cover the road at a rate of perhaps 15 miles a day. A quick jaunt down Route 40 in Pennsylvania, which follows the path of the original National Road, will give some sense of how tough those horses must have had it. There was no attempt to, in the words of the country song, straighten the curves and flatten the hills. The road follows the geometry of the geology. When it was built, it was not possible to do otherwise.

Yet the National Road had one advantage: Thanks to the fledgling power of the federal government, it was built in a straight line wherever money or legislation could make it so. The gravel tributaries that departed the main route had no such advantage. Even today they duck, sweep, and dive across boundaries of property and influence that have long since vanished into the history books.

The Federal-Aid Highway Act of 1956 reimagined the American road along the lines of the prewar German autobahn, bringing with it standards of construction that seem designed to destroy that cherished variety. The maximum permitted grade is six percent; the "design speed" is 70 mph, but the vehicles used to determine that speed are now primarily found at vintage car shows or rusting away in farmers' fields. Unfortunately, American construction standards are not quite up to German standards. The autobahn typically consists of two concrete layers on a crushed limestone base; American freeways are often a single layer of concrete or even asphalt on a bed of sand, with expansion joints spaced farther apart in the interest of saving cost.

Cheaper the roads might be, but little expense was spared in making the landscape conform to their design specs. The construction of I-70, which parallels the National Road, involved tremendous mechanized effort and an unknown but doubtless considerable amount of dynamite. The newer I-68 is even more ambitious, chopping mountains down to size and bridging dozens of gaps in an effort to bring more uniformity to the road surface. Still, the alert driver on I-68 will see a few exits marked "US-40." Those are for the old road, which climbs the mountains that its descendant carelessly flattened. It's possible to take one of those exits, spend a half hour at full throttle on hairpin passes rivaling anything in Italy, then rejoin I-68 two miles down the road. Consider it a litmus test for driving enthusiasm, easy to take and conclusive in its results.

TWO ROADS, *both alike in dignity / in fair Robbinsville, where we lay our scene.*

TripAdvisor tells us there are 15 great things to do and see in this North Carolina town of approximately 620 residents. Zip lines. A forest named after Joyce Kilmer. A locally owned store that sells honey. Yet the casual observer would be forgiven for thinking Robbinsville is next door to a racetrack. On sunny days there is a constant flow of wheeled machinery through the main-street gas-station lanes and drive-through restaurants. Motorcycles range from race replica to aftermarket "retirement trikes," the latter built from Harleys and Gold Wings for riders who are no longer strong or confident enough to hold up a standard bike at stoplights. Dozens of Mazda Miatas in various states of tune display a diverse seriousness of intent.

Some of the cars don't look quite street legal, because they aren't. They arrive huddled inside anonymous trailers and are released into the twilight to serve their single purpose: setting a point-to-point record on an 11-mile section of U.S. Route 129. It's called the "Tail of the Dragon," and although you won't find the demarcation points on any official map, it's commonly understood to start at the Cheoah Dam in North Carolina and end at the Tabcat Creek Bridge in Tennessee. Between those two points, there are about 318 curves.

Robbinsville is the nearest town to the Dragon's starting line. Here you can meet the broad spectrum of riders and drivers who have come from all over the world to try this road for themselves, the retired couples on their 900-pound "rolling sofas" and the young men in their snarling Mitsubishi Evos. You can find someone to show you the road at a relaxed pace, pointing out the photographers who make a living by snapping every single vehicle that passes and putting their shots up for sale on various websites. You can get someone to be your "rabbit" and help you improve your pace over each of those 318 corners. You can even lay a friendly bet on the outcome of a point-by-point race, with the usual caveats of what will happen if you are stymied by an Electra Glide doing sightseeing duty or a crunched convertible straddling the road at the least convenient moment.

Grimes Canyon Road, Fillmore, California.
Photo by Richard Pardon

What you *won't* find: the best of the best, the elite drivers who have made it their life's mission to set the lowest possible time on the Dragon. They operate in the secret spaces of time and road created by the natural rhythms of tourist presence and police enforcement. The "lap times" they set are known only to a select few.

Matt Chambers is one of them. His garage, which boasts multiple 600-plus-hp supercars, would be a track rat's dream, but like Hunter S. Thompson, he cares little for the antiseptic security of a closed course. For more than a quarter century, he's been perfecting his personal approach to Route 129. Yet it was not until 2014 that he had a chance to test himself against the fastest of those shadowy locals in a private meeting that had the gravitas of an underground martial-arts tournament and the festive atmosphere of an impromptu race party.

"I kept waiting for them to pick up the pace," he says, "but they never did." Encouraged by the feet of clay his heroes displayed on the road's fastest corners, Chambers would go on to record a series of breathtaking timed runs that many say are the fastest "laps" the Dragon has ever seen. In the course of doing so, he came into contact with the separate-but-equal subculture of legendary sports bikers who are also engaged in a furious battle to set the lowest possible time. "The bikes can't match our speed," Chambers notes, "and the best of them have crashed again and again trying to narrow the gap to the cars. The two best riders out there finally gave up and retired. The risk got to be too much."

Having recently added some remarkable weapons-grade hardware to his fleet, Chambers is far from letting his own obsession go. "There's more time out there. You have to approach the limit strategically. I've never crashed there, because I'm on the hook for my own expenses if I wreck a car. If we could close it off for a day, that would be ideal."

What makes this particular ribbon of tarmac so compelling anyway? "For me," Chambers replies, "it's the folklore, the legend of the place, and the road itself. When you're going for time, you can never relax. There's never a point in your run where you can say it's all gravy after this. Route 129 will challenge you from beginning to end."

MAYBE THAT'S WHY NO ROAD IN AMERICA quite carries the Dragon's cachet. It isn't close to being the fastest or most challenging two-lane in the country. It's not even the most exciting road passing through Robbinsville, North Carolina. That honor would go to the Cherohala Skyway, which departs from Route 129 and heads west just north of the city.

Its name is a portmanteau of Cherokee and Nantahala, the two national forests crossed by the skyway over its 41 desolate and elevated miles. Developed at a cost of more than $100 million, the Cherohala winds up and over a series of mountains to heights of about 5400 feet, without so much as a single gas station or general store to interrupt the road's flow. The scenery is hugely varied: crystal-clear lakes surrounded by evergreens, long sweeps across the crests of hills with distant vistas to all sides, sheer drops into the valleys below.

Like the Dragon, the Cherohala has hundreds of corners and no shortage of challenge for the driver. Yet it is nearly deserted most days, even as its famous neighbor develops what locals call "conga lines" of ponderously paced traffic. What's the difference? Why is one of Robbinsville's mountain roads globally famous while the other remains strictly for the cognoscenti?

There are a few obvious answers. The Cherohala has a shorter season; its greater elevation and long stretches where there is no tree cover to tame the mountain wind can lead to black ice and slippery conditions as late as April and as early as November. Unlike the Dragon, there's no infrastructure of tourist services, restaurants, and photography stations along its length—but Route 129 had none of that stuff 25 years ago, when it first started gaining notoriety in enthusiast publications and on the fledgling internet. Last but not least, the Dragon is about one-quarter the length and is therefore easier for its drivers to memorize and fully exploit at speed, although Matt Chambers claims that, unlike some of the other "kings" of the road, he has never bothered to become more than "pretty much familiar" with the precise order of corners. "You can usually see what's next."

None of that matters as much as a simple fact that will become apparent to any trained driver who tries both roads in succession: Compared with Route 129, the Cherohala is simply *too fast*. Even the most committed and talented Dragon slayers will rarely exceed 90 mph between turns, but the Cherohala has dozens of sections where powerful sports cars can easily double that velocity. It doesn't help that there is little to no room for error on the road's fastest and highest stretches.

A no-holds-barred drive on the Dragon can be exhilarating, but running to the Cherohala's limit usually produces emotions closer to terror, even in the recollection. There is no secret society of midnight runners who probe its limits. When a local paper asked for comment on fatalities on the two roads, a North Carolina trooper attributed the Dragon's casualties to "inattention." The Cherohala's victims? "Speed."

Which leads us to a revelation that can be more than a little uncomfortable for people who, like Hunter S. Thompson, prided themselves on being street racers: In addition to scenery and variety, a first-rate driving road needs approachability. There is such a thing as too big, and such a thing as too fast.

Chambers agrees. "I'm seeing maybe 100 mph on the fastest stretches of the Dragon," he says, "with an overall average right at 60 mph. On the Cherohala, you're doing 150, 160, with more to come. If the Dragon is like a fast autocross course, then the Cherohala is more like a big track, something like Willow Springs. Except with no guardrails and no safety margin whatsoever. I don't find it compelling. Not at those speeds."

The reticence on the part of even the Dragon's fastest drivers is, I think, a good thing, because it offers an overdue no-fault divorce between the driver's enthusiasm and the showoff's machismo. It leaves the rest of us free to concentrate on the experiences that make a road truly great: the ebb and flow of the turns, the way the terrain engages and challenges the driver without endangering or confusing, the space and time necessary to enter that relaxed state where the cares of past and present disappear.

An hour on the right road can seem to pass in minutes, and it can justify hours' worth of transit time to get there. You don't need the fastest car, and you don't need to set any point-to-point records. When the right ribbon of tarmac unfolds before you, quality has a quantity all its own.

ON MY FIRST AND ONLY TRIP TO THE DRAGON, I started in Robbinsville and ended up at the infamous "Tree of Shame," where the branches and roots are decorated with the detritus of a thousand motorcycle crashes, dangling brake levers, and crumpled bodywork. It wasn't deliberate, and I wasn't alone. I met my companion for the trip at one of the few gas stations near the Dragon's starting line. He was a young man in factory-fresh leathers on a polished Suzuki GSX-R750, surrounded by hangers-on and lesser lights; I was a middle-aged fellow in a mid-engine Porsche designed for the midlife crisis.

"Sure, I can show you the fast way through the Dragon," he laughed. "You can pay for my gas and a drink after. You ain't gonna be close after the first mile or so, though." The crowd laughed with him reflexively. I handed him a $20, and we set off. He was at the front of his superbike flock, and I was tailing at a respectful 100-foot distance.

On the way there, he and his friends played good-natured games of intimidation with me, wheelieing away while my silver convertible gasped breathlessly behind. Past the bridge, his posse formed a line behind him, and we attacked the Dragon in earnest.

His prediction came true almost immediately. I lost sight of him in the first few corners. Ah, but here's the thing about the Dragon: Its mostly flat curves are an exercise in flat g-loading. On a motorcycle, it's exhausting work, but in a sports car with aroma-fresh, 235-width, high-performance tires up front and 265-width rubber in back, the road is an exercise in what famed racing instructor Ross Bentley calls "library matching." You look at each curve as you approach it, then you think back through every curve you've ever driven, and you select a speed that feels like 95 percent of the possible, and you sail through in a dust-raising, rubber-squeaky slide.

About three miles in, I started passing one or two of his hangers-on every time the corner exit offered several hundred feet of clear vision. A few would try to repass on the next turn entry, but a sports bike doesn't outbrake a Porsche, not when the fall leaves are starting to paper the tarmac. They would raise the front wheel behind me in impotent fury and then fade out of the mirror in a few turns.

Slightly past the halfway point, I came up behind my tour guide. He had the true gift that distinguishes brilliant motorcyclists from the merely competent—the authentic lightness of touch. The Suzuki appeared to be mounted on ceramic-bearing gimbals as it leaned into each turn. You could put a slip of paper between his knee and the road but perhaps not two of them.

Finally, the road opened up, and on a fourth-gear turn, I laid off the brake a moment longer than was prudent, flashing my headlights in his mirror as I did. He responded by carrying a tiny fraction more speed than the laws of physics would permit. The Suzuki slid out from under him, and the crash-guard pegs affixed to its frame sent bright sparks into the air before a cloud of gravel dust enveloped bike and rider. I hit my hazards and pulled over.

He was standing with his helmet off before I could get out of the car, wide-eyed and nervously laughing. Together we collected the pieces of bodywork that were strewn along the road. His friends arrived and collaborated on some field repair to get the GSX-R up and running. The forks were twisted and the bike had acquired an embarrassingly skeletal aspect after its forcible undressing. It still ran well enough to reach 45 or so mph.

"Can you hold on to some of this stuff?" he asked, handing me a pile of shredded plastic. "I never thought this would happen, but I need to go to the Tree. You know what I'm talking about. The Tree of Shame. Let's go there together, man. I guess I mighta took you too light. Or maybe I took myself too heavy. Either way." Then we formed a funeral procession behind him and traveled at the legal limit or below, my Porsche hazards blinking at the tail of it in an attempt to ward off whatever faster traffic might appear without warning.

That was how we went to the Tree. Although 13 long and occasionally painful years have passed between then and now, I often think of that slow trip back along the Dragon, and I never think of our combined arrogance and foolishness without feeling a little shame of my own.

Bixby Creek Bridge, Highway 1, Big Sur, California.
Photo by Richard Pardon

If you look hard enough, chances are you'll eventually find an escape road of your own.

9 / IT'S NOT ABOUT THE CAR

It was very hot and a terribly difficult race. Ayrton had a bit of a mixed bag: He'd qualified all right, thought the car was okay. He'd spun early in the race and had to work his way back but was heading toward a reasonable if not stunning finish. Then he clipped the wall, damaged a wheel, and broke a driveshaft. After the race he was distraught and really couldn't understand how he'd hit the wall. We were sitting talking, debriefing, and he said: "It's impossible I hit the wall. The wall moved."

I said, "Yeah, sure it did." They were huge great concrete blocks. But he was so insistent, and I had so much confidence in the guy, that I said, "Okay, we've just got to go and look at this." I did think he was talking bollocks, but he needed to go and see it. So we walked out to where he'd hit the wall, and do you know what? The wall had moved. It was made of the great big concrete blocks they used to delineate the circuit, but what happened was someone had hit the far end of a block and pushed it, which made the leading edge come out a few millimeters. He was driving with such precision that those few millimeters, and I'm talking probably 10 millimeters, were enough for him to hit the wall that time rather than just miss it.

That really opened my eyes. I knew the guy was good, but that really told me how special. Not just the driving but this conviction, the analysis, and then the conclusion: I cannot be wrong, so the wall must have moved. *Everyone else would say, "Bollocks, how on earth did I do that?" But the conviction he had was staggering. And he was right.*

Ayrton Senna, U.S. Grand Prix, 1991. *Photo by Mike Powell, Allsport/Getty Images*

—FORMULA 1 ENGINEER PAT SYMONDS, ON MULTIPLE WORLD CHAMPION AYRTON SENNA

(TONY DODGINS, *AYRTON SENNA: ALL HIS RACES*, EVRO PUBLISHING, 2014)

You quickly realize there aren't any gods in racing.

—SIXTEEN-TIME SPORTS-CAR CHAMPION
AND LEGENDARY GM ENGINEER JOHN HEINRICY

WHICH CAME FIRST, the automobile or the automobile race? It was the former, albeit barely. Brothers Charles and Frank Duryea made America's first usable gasoline-powered automobile in 1893; about a year and a half later, they lined up against five competitors for America's first official four-wheel motorsport event, which they won, handily. In racing, then as now, a little technological head start goes a long way.

The automobile *racing driver,* by contrast, trailed the automobile *race* by decades. And why not? The earliest racing cars didn't exactly require the sure hands of a Mario Andretti. They weren't nearly as fast as a steam-powered locomotive, they possessed no dynamic qualities of braking or handling above those of the horse-drawn carriages from which they were derived, and they broke down more often than they ran. The most critical skill a driver could possess in that era was mechanical aptitude. Even in the contests where ride-along mechanics were permitted, it made sense to have four hands working on the car instead of two.

The first and most famous driver from the prewar era, Barney Oldfield, had the same résumé as many of his fellow competitors: converted board-track cyclist. It wasn't until the first decade of the 20th century that the idea of a professional automobile race-car driver began to acquire any currency. Even after it did, the focus for most spectators remained squarely on the machinery in question. The "win on Sunday, sell on Monday" philosophy found its early expression in the public cross-country races staged here in the States and in Europe, with an emphasis on reliability, not outright speed. The former was much more important to prospective customers than the latter. There were few roads where an automobile might be able to maintain double-digit speeds for any length of time, but if your Duryea or Ford came to a halt, you would most likely have to fix it yourself. The pioneer driver out on a motoring adventure would likely agree with an aphorism favored by today's international investors: The *fact* of return is of much greater concern than the rate of return.

This idea of racing as an extended demonstration of product or even political virtue (the Nazi-backed Grand Prix machines of the Thirties, for example) lasted until a wave of post–World War II prosperity produced a generation of people interested in competition for its own sake. Although the motivations were presumably identical, the outlets for those motivations were determined somewhat ironically by the differing philosophies of governance in Europe and America. On the Continent, it was considered perfectly normal to close the roads and make the proles wait while dashing aristocrats clashed in events like the Mille Miglia in Italy. In the States, however, that sort of thing was frowned on for reasons of egalitarianism, so the American racing scene developed instead on oval tracks designed for horse and dog racing. And that, in a nutshell, is why Europe's premier race is the Monaco Grand Prix and America's greatest spectacle is the Indianapolis 500.

This is not to say that road racing, in its original form, didn't get a foothold here, helped by two separate but complementary developments in the Anglo-American "special relationship" during and after the war. The first was the unprecedented exposure of GIs, in Europe, to the middle-class English sports car as exemplified by the MG Midget TC. There was no direct equivalent to these small-bore specials in the U.S., thanks to an American tax code that didn't penalize displacement or horsepower in the same manner as did the exchequer of Great Britain. The United States had big, fast expensive cars from Duesenberg and the like. We had working-class heroes like the flathead Ford. But an affordable two-seater designed specifically for *la vie sportive?* To a group of young people with money in their pockets and a yen for postwar adventure, the MG and its immediate competitors were irresistible.

Just as important was the English government's "export or die" policy of the late Forties and early Fifties. Desperate for hard currency to balance the books of Lend-Lease and repair the depredations of the Blitz, Clement Attlee's Labour Party ministries employed a variety of rationing strategies for steel, iron, rubber, and oil. The only way for a private corporation to get its hands on these materials was to commit to an export-focused strategy. In 1950, British automakers produced just over half a million cars. Nearly 400,000 of those were shipped to America.

Compared with our homegrown offerings, these British cars were remarkably expensive and lamentably slow. Nevertheless, they found enthusiastic customers in former service members who had admired them during time overseas. Those ex-GIs, in turn, found a home in a rebooted Sports Car Club of America, which had returned from a wartime hiatus and redefined itself as a fairly exclusive club for owners of upscale and foreign sporting cars built after 1914.

Then, as now, SCCA members looked for opportunities to exercise their mettle and metal. The timed hill climb, brought over from the U.K. as a cult expression of Continental competition, comprised a majority of the club's early activities. It didn't satisfy the would-be wheel-to-wheel racers in the club, but the idea of running MGs and Jowetts on the dirt ovals outside most Midwestern towns didn't satisfy the aristocratic impulses of the SCCA's early leaders. The solution was to follow the European road-course model, modified for American tastes.

A glance through the 1953 SCCA National schedule shows a couple of hill climbs and one asphalt oval, but the majority of events were held on newly idled air force bases with the runways barricaded to form primitive racetracks. This arrangement was a product of, and nicely symbolic of, the club's transition from blue-blood fraternity to serviceman's competitive outlet. It wouldn't last. The Cold War and the Red scares of the Fifties would restrict access to those venues; meanwhile, the growing skill and speed of those early club racers resulted in demands for increased variety and greater challenge on-track.

Thus, the purpose-built American road course was born. It didn't happen all at once, as shown by the history of one event in New York's Finger Lakes region. In 1948, Cameron Argetsinger persuaded the town of Watkins Glen to shut down for the day and let him stage an SCCA event. Impressively, he convinced the New York Central Railroad to hold traffic on the rail that crossed his makeshift course. The race was considered a success, leading to subsequent annual events. A driver's death in 1950 didn't unduly deter the participants, but an accident in 1952 that injured 12 spectators and killed one brought a swift end to the original "track" layout.

The race resumed the following year on a course laid out using farming roads away from the town proper. It wasn't popular with drivers or spectators, so Argetsinger and the race's other organizers created a purpose-built track in 1956. That facility, with various additions and changes for safety and logistics, has survived to the current day. This progression from road course to "road course" was repeated dozens of times here and in Europe throughout the Fifties and Sixties.

Club racing has always been uniquely susceptible to economic downturns; it's ruinously expensive and often practiced by people who can barely afford to put tires on their cars. ("If you want to make a small fortune in racing," as the saying goes, "start with a large one.") Yet SCCA regions and various marque clubs have managed to bounce back from this country's last major recession, putting hundreds of cars on grids a dozen or so times every year. What drives the weekend warrior? It can be many things: a desire to emulate the heroes of the USAC or IMSA circuits, a stubborn affection for a particular car or marque, a generic need for speed that is only satisfied in wheel-to-wheel competition.

To its most affectionate practitioners, club racing becomes more than a way of life; it becomes the glue that holds the rest of their days together. For Phil Alspach—an 80-year-old SCCA road racer who has been consistently involved in his SCCA region across six decades and who can still be found at the club's national-championship Runoffs— it's nothing less than the engine that motivates him to stay healthy and active.

"I started this racing thing pretty late in life," Phil says, crinkling his eyes so I know he's not entirely serious. He was 21 when he began participating in early unsanctioned autocrosses on the grounds of the Ohio State University. Nine years later, in 1968, he joined the SCCA and began competing in the Solo II program. "Then," he notes, "I realized I could run my Triumph in the road races as well. It was my street driver, my autocross car, and my road-race car for Nationals. Of course, you don't see that flexibility as much nowadays—if at all."

Phil's house serves multiple roles: It's the garage where he maintains his collection of four club race cars; it's a museum containing hundreds of framed racing photos and stacks of trophies from across the country; it's a warehouse of sorts for the Ohio Valley Region where Phil is still an active club executive. On this particular day, the living room has 20 boxes containing the trophies for Mid-Ohio's June Sprints, a race in which he and I are entered. "I suppose," he drawls, "I could give you an advance look at 'em." Behind those boxes is a cut-crystal Lifetime Achievement Award from OVR-SCCA honoring his 50 years of service as a volunteer and administrator.

"I ran 15 years of the Runoffs," Alspach says, "and I finished every one. I didn't win any, but I always finished. In '74, I took second at [the SCCA's autocross championship] Solo Nationals. But I've always done it on the cheap. You won't get anywhere if you do it on the cheap." He pauses. "Ten years ago, I was diagnosed with thyroid cancer. Had it removed in 2009. The medication takes a lot out of you. I get tired easy. For that reason, I like the shorter races now. I like to start aggressively, run down the outside going into Turn One at Mid-Ohio. Most of the time, it's decided in the first six or seven laps. Then you're just waiting for someone to break, or they're waiting for you to break."

After more than 600 SCCA starts, Phil has become well-known for the regularity with which he competes and volunteers at Mid-Ohio. "I don't like to miss a race there." Sure enough, reviewing my own SCCA race records, I see he's been present for every single event in which I competed, and quite a few others besides.

"At my age, with these old cars I'm running, I don't often have a lot of direct competition. But you're still in there with everybody else, still in the race." His 1994 Dodge Neon, purchased new by him and raced in the early years of the Neon Challenge against luminaries such as Bob Lutz and Denise McCluggage, sits forlorn in his driveway, a patchwork of SCCA stickers covering up spots where paint has long since declared independence from primer. Although he's reluctant to admit it, Phil

1949 MG TC, Watkins Glen, New York. *Photo courtesy the REVS Institute*

1965 Mustang, Elkhart Lake, Wisconsin. *Photo by Richard Pardon*

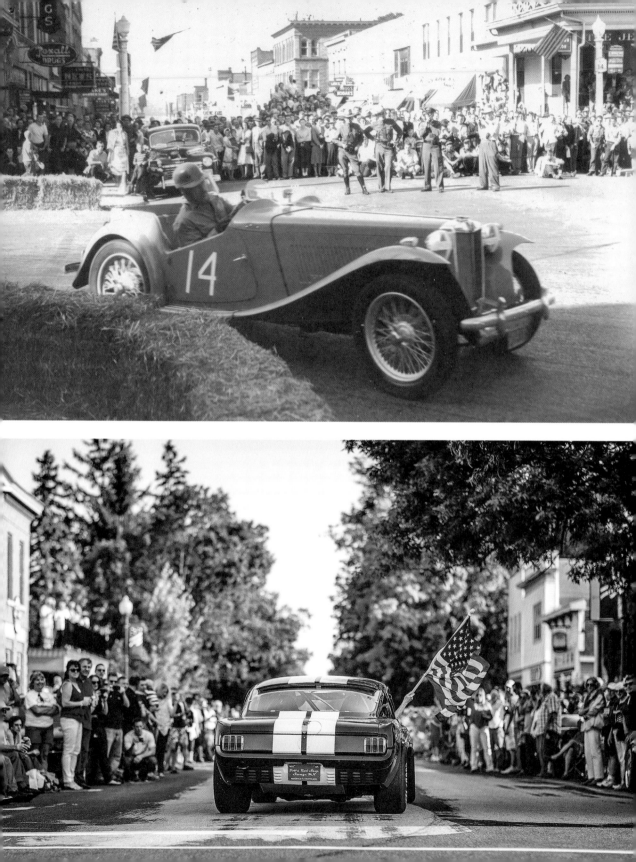

still has a few goals left as a road racer. "I want to get my RX-7 down to, say, 1:45 on the Mid-Ohio Club Course. I'm at 1:49 now. This year I changed brake compounds. I might even get new tires. A second is not a long time. You make changes, and you get that second. Then you make more changes and you get another one. Sometimes you can't tell if it's you or the car that stands between you and the time you want. Well, most of the time, it's you. But it can be the car, too."

Like many club racers, Phil is a racing fan as well. "Paul Newman was an inspiration to me. Mark Donohue, as well. A few years ago, I was on the grid with Graham Rahal. I told him not to hit me when he came around the lapped traffic." Tucked among the dozens of framed photos from his races over the past decades, I see some of the original promotional material for the movie *Grand Prix*. "That one, they got right. *Le Mans*, too. The new one—*Rush*—that's really good."

Remarkably, Phil still operates a side business mounting tires on an old-school hydraulic machine on his back patio. To watch him ease a stubborn Hoosier radial onto a wire wheel is to doubt he will ever run out of energy and ability to race. Yet he's sanguine about what's ahead. "At some point," he admits as he walks me out, past his brace of RX-7s, "they're going to take my license away. You can't race forever. There is such a thing as being too old. Well, when that happens," and now his eyes are crinkling in earnest, "maybe I'll try that track-day thing that everybody's so excited about."

Drivers like Phil and his 40,000 or so fellow travelers in club racing are more than weekend warriors searching for the meaning of life in home-welded safety cages at 130 mph. They are also the custodians of a unique progression of automobile racing from product demonstration to sporting event. Yes, the spectator-driven tradition still survives in America, most notably with NASCAR's traveling circus and its feeder series. Beyond that, there are still dozens of small towns across the country where Friday-night circle-track races draw profitable crowds to watch everything from stripped-out Chevy Cavaliers to elaborately festooned school buses.

If you look at the new facilities built over the past couple of decades, however, they are increasingly hewing to a single template: the "country club" track focused on the amateur competitor and enthusiast. Unlike Watkins Glen, Laguna Seca, or Mid-Ohio, these are constructed without any expectation of, or accommodation for, throngs of passive spectators. The best views are reserved for million-dollar "garage mahals" constructed by wealthy individuals a few hundred feet off the racing surface; the rest of the spectator areas look suspiciously like empty fields.

You can blame, or credit, the rise of the track day for this phenomenon. On one hand, it's a democratization of access to the racetrack. Prior to about 20 years ago, you needed to be an accredited racer with the SCCA or a marque organization like the BMW Car Club of America to drive a car at speed on a road course. That all changed shortly before the turn of the century, when a for-profit venture called NASA and a few other groups started renting out tracks and offering "driver education" programs, where regular Joes and Janes could take their street-legal Porsche or Hyundai for a high-speed weekend.

The country-club track is a natural consequence of this new paradigm, offering its members a chance to drive their high-performance cars at high speed at their convenience the same way they might enjoy 18 holes on a Wednesday afternoon. IndyCar veteran Ross Bentley is at the forefront of a movement aimed at teaching these casual drivers a modified form of racecraft, one applicable to driving that is not explicitly competitive but still capable of stirring the blood for those who need a stronger hit of adrenaline than they can reliably, or legally, obtain on a public road.

"The same techniques from racing apply to track days," Bentley says. "You're still working with your own limits and the limits of the car. The difference is how serious you're going to be about it. I guess I should also say that some of the 'noncompetitive' drivers are extremely competitive about their lap times, and about passing other drivers."

Still, if the desire for competition is what separates the club rat from the country-club driver, what separates the committed amateur from the professional sports-car drivers who fill the ranks of IMSA, Pirelli World Challenge, and a few other spectator-oriented American series?

And what, in turn, separates them from the elite cadre of full-time pros who run million-dollar prototypes for automakers like Audi and Porsche at Le Mans and elsewhere?

Not everybody believes there *is* a difference. John Heinricy, the General Motors engineer and multiple amateur- and pro-series champion who's quoted on page 124, is an example of the journeymen who believe they can compete at any level—and who occasionally do. There's a remarkable amount of cross-pollination between the upper levels of amateur competition and everyday pro racing; a Venn diagram created from the average SCCA Runoffs entrant list and an IMSA event program would contain a nontrivial amount of overlap.

There's a general consensus, however, that the best pro drivers have something you can't learn, or retain, by running a half-dozen club races every year. Maybe it's an extra few tenths of a second around a dangerous, challenging course like Spa in Belgium. It could be a unique ability for overtaking or defending in the darkening hours of a 24-hour endurance race. Or it could be a sense of leadership that unites the team in a way that a "spank"—what pro teams call self-funded drivers, as opposed to those who pay for their seats through sponsorship—just can't manage.

"At every level," Bentley likes to say, "you are a team leader." Consider, again, Michael Schumacher. He was never considered the greatest talent on the grid, nor was he lauded for extraordinary car control. Yet he understood the telos of racing, the organic whole of competition, a comprehension that started with his ability to remember the name of every crew member in a 200-person F1 team and ended with his multihour workouts *after* enduring the physical rigors of a two-hour race. In the car, as well, he demonstrated an uncanny ability to strategize on the fly and understand the strategies of the other teams, even as he operated a vehicle that rivaled an F-16 in its ability to stress the human body.

Schumacher's unique abilities have not been duplicated since, but the best pro drivers in any series need to possess at least a rough facsimile of his attitude and approach. Today's racers face something their

1910 Fiat S76, the Beast of Turin. *Photo by Richard Pardon*

1965 Shelby Mustang GT350 and 1963 Shelby Cobra, Laguna Seca Raceway, California. *Photo by Matt Tierney*

predecessors never considered: the advent of a driver-training industry that can give 45-year-old, independently wealthy rookies the ability to closely shade the youth karting virtuosos and open-wheel standouts with whom they share an IMSA prototype or GT-class supercar.

In the postwar era, drivers like Bob Bondurant and Carroll Shelby would change the line they took through a turn when another car was behind them, just to keep their secrets from wider distribution. Today, a rookie driver can expect that he or she will have access to exhaustively comprehensive data from experienced pros—and that the rookie, in turn, will have to share that data with team strategists.

There is no longer anywhere to hide, a fact obvious even when dipping a toe into the waters of professional motorsports. Ten years ago, I ran my first pro race in Grand Am's Koni Challenge with the team that would take the season championship that year. I knew I'd have to match the team pros for pace and fuel economy. What I didn't expect was that the team would be able to measure everything I was doing in the car, from brake-pedal pressure to the millimeter-precise motions of the suspension. The difference between me and the series champion wasn't expressed in abstract concepts like heart or vision or guts. It was detailed in a spreadsheet I had to study between practice sessions until I got my act together. I'd expected to be Steve McQueen in *Le Mans;* what I got instead was a combination of pep talk and tax audit.

The summer before writing these words, I drove the first examples of the 2019 Corvette for *Road & Track* magazine. I spent the day with the team that engineered the car and in the process discovered the Corvette now has all the measurement abilities of an IMSA racer. Do you want to know how your suspension travel through Virginia International Raceway's infamous climbing esses compares with that of a pro driver or engineer? Just pull the SD card from the Corvette's infotainment system, plug it into your laptop, and fire up the software package from Cosworth Engineering that's provided free of charge with every new Corvette—from the fire-breathing ZR1 track monster to the automatic-transmission convertibles driven by Florida retirees.

Another surprise: The ZR1, like its competitors from exotic houses such as Ferrari and Lamborghini, offers more power than the similarly shaped race cars in various pro series. The McLaren 570S GT4, which competes in IMSA's Continental Tire Challenge, is about 150 horses down on the roadgoing McLaren 570S you can buy at your local dealership. This is no accident. Modern cars are so powerful that they threaten to overwhelm the safety precautions built into even the newest country-club tracks. For the first time in history, daily-driven vehicles are more technologically advanced than even the newest race cars. With a few exceptions, such as the supercomputer-designed aerodynamic packages of Formula 1 cars—generally estimated to be a full 20 years ahead of today's front-line fighter jets—the race car has to be content to trail the breed, not improve it.

Here's the thing: It doesn't really matter. As thrilling as it might be to operate a 1000-hp hypercar at its 200-mph limit, that's light beer compared with the moonshine rush of wheel-to-wheel competition. It doesn't matter if you're in the cockpit of a Le Mans prototype or strapped into the $150 bent-aluminum seat of a weekend-rental Spec Miata. When you see that green flag wave, you immediately undergo a sort of reversible lobotomy. Everything from your mortgage payment to your lingering self-doubts about your ability—it all vanishes. For the duration of that race, you and your car are a flesh-and-metal hybrid with one purpose: Get ahead of the bumper in front of you, and the next one, and the one after that. Every sense is heightened, every moment freighted with the immense weight of competitive significance.

In those moments, there's room for bravery or even greatness that nobody but you will ever see. Your foot might hover over the brake for a critical half-second extra. That could win you a plastic trophy, or it could put you into a concrete wall at 100 mph. The back end of your car will step out in a way that would freeze your blood on a snowy winter-morning commute, but here you will correct it with a flicker and impassively note that it brought your fender within a finger's width of the car next to you. You will strategize as you size up the driver ahead and then act with a sort of decisiveness that feels foreign anywhere but down the back straight of your home track.

Afterward, in the long cooldown lap after the checkered flag, or perhaps packing up in the paddock, you will return to your everyday self. It's not a pleasant process. To paraphrase John Updike: After being a racing driver, a businessman's skin feels tight. The club rats talk about track withdrawal symptoms as if they were discussing the first day an addict spends away from the needle. They aren't far off. What you want is to shed your skin and snake your way into another pregrid—the sooner, the better.

Maybe John Heinricy is right. Maybe there are no gods in racing. Or maybe there *are* gods in racing, and maybe we race because it is the closest we ever come to that divinity. Maybe we race for the moments where you feel a fleeting kinship with a driver who could pass a concrete block at vision-blurring speed and notice it had moved a fraction of an inch. Or maybe we race to be our own heroes.

"I started this whole thing kind of late," Phil Alspach told me, after we had examined his trophies and photos and commiserated over the ability of a rotary engine to turn you from race leader to spectator in a heartless half second. "After 50 years, though, I think it's safe to say it's kind of my life."

Trans-Am race cars at the Monterey Historics in 2012.
Photo by Evan Klein

Drifting BY SAM POSEY

My first encounter with a driftable car came at Lime Rock the year before I turned 21 and could get a license. In the meantime, I was hanging around the pits hoping some nice driver would let me do a few laps in his car. Well, a few actually did, but not enough. So for $1000 I bought my own car, a Jocko. Actually, I should say *the* Jocko because it was the only one.

It was a Formula Junior, which was a hot class at the time—despite the unfortunate name. The cars were a lot like the F1 cars of the day, except smaller and a good deal slower. The Jocko's builder was Jocko Maggiacomo of Pough-keepsie, New York. He had pulled a driver from a burning car at Sebring and was a certified hero. But his car didn't live up to his reputation. One conspicuous failing was the solid rear axle, which he took out of a sprint car, and the car was 200 pounds too heavy. The driveshaft also ran directly under the seat. Other than that, it was a step toward Formula 1.

My hero was Juan Manuel Fangio—a five-time world champion, and the undisputed master of the drift. In 1957, drifting in F1 reached its apogee with Fangio driving a Maserati in practice for the French GP at Reims.

The first turn at the end of the pit straight was a fast, lethal right-hand sweeper that had deep ditches on both sides and no guardrails. Lap after lap Fangio came by with the tail far out and the front wheels flicking one way and then the other, all four wheels in play, the car dancing on its thin tires and tiny contact patches with a delicacy that suggested ballet. But there was violence, too, with the sight of the onrushing red machine cocked at an angle across the narrow road—the heat, the noise, the smell of Castrol oil.

It was almost like that in the Jocko—the accurate pointing of the car at the apex, the hood stretching out ahead. Drifting! I wasn't Fangio, but I could do the same thing he did, with less precision. I had the car for a month until, finally, I couldn't ignore the thought that the driveshaft would seize up somehow and lash around right where I was sitting, and I sold it.

The car was gone, but the dreams stayed with me, and for a moment just before the 1972 Formula 5000 season, they came back to life. My team was negotiating with a potential sponsor, and we decided to wow them with a picture of the car at full opposite lock. While testing at Ontario, we had a free-lance photographer set up at a sharp right-hander where I threw the car into

Above: Posey before the Minnesota Grand Prix, July 1972. Photo by Bill Eppridge

Opposite: Fangio, 1957 French Grand Prix. Photo by Louis Klemantaski

an exaggerated slide that, after a few tries, I managed to turn into an actual drift. We sent the picture off to the sponsor and got the deal. Pleased with ourselves, we sent another photo to John Surtees, from whom we had bought the car. By then, the tires were so wide and grippy that the most efficient use of them did not call for the slip angles necessary in a drift. Unhappily, Big John took us seriously and said the photo was one of the dumbest he'd ever seen.

One of my strangest experiences with drifting was driving a car designed by the great Colin Chapman of Lotus fame. The car was for Indy and had features specific to the 500—a turbine engine, four-wheel drive, and a distinctive wedge shape. Chapman built three of them, and they were the class of the field. One, driven by Joe Leonard, nearly won. After the 500, a contractual agreement with Chrysler saw the turbines replaced with its stock-block V-8s. But testing on the road course didn't go well, and team members feared they would be uncompetitive on the road courses that made up most of the remaining races. They decided the blame rested with Joe Leonard and offered me the ride.

The last race of the season was Seattle, and I was dueling with Dan Gurney. In the rain, with four-wheel drive and my superior Firestone tires (Dan was on Goodyears), I was able to drift the car through the fast turns while he fought to catch slides before they began. This unfair advantage, I thought, was what Dan must feel every other race.

In road racing, drifting by then was nearly an obsolete skill. But the heart of the experience certainly lives on: the challenges and rewards of taking a car to the limit.

Sam Posey competed at racing's highest levels before turning to broadcasting, writing, and painting.

PART FOUR | BY **BRETT BERK**

The Life

LIVING WITH THE CAR
WHILE CHASING THE WORLD OUTSIDE IT.

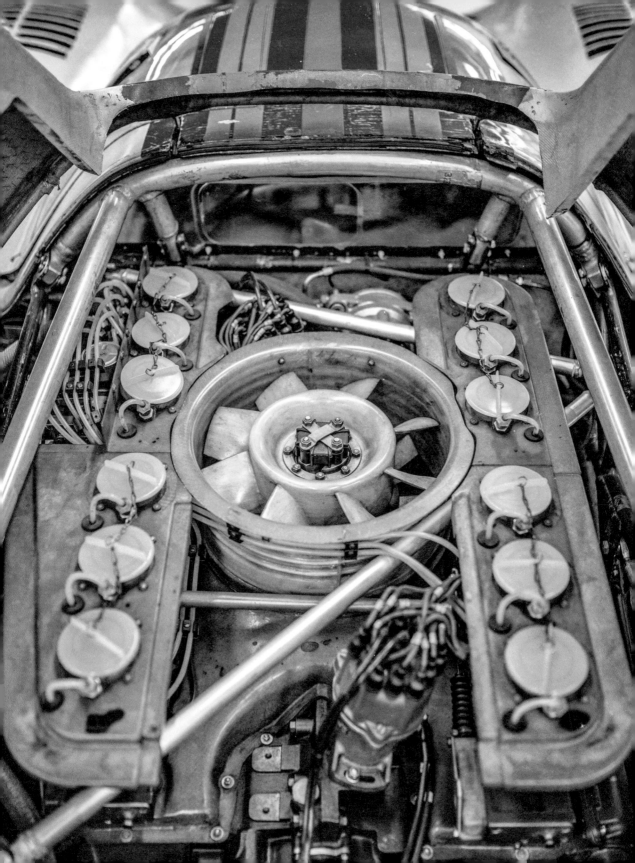

10/ ARCHAEOLOGY

THE AUTOMOBILE MIGHT BE THE MOST IMPORTANT mechanical artifact of the 20th century. It strongly influenced the design of our modern environment of roads and interstates, bridges and tunnels, urban planning, housing, and retail establishments. Moreover, it impacted nearly every element of our national psyche, from our notions of independence, escapism, and adventure, to the plots and subjects of film, television, literature, and design. Yet the car is not typically accorded the kind of consideration or analysis afforded to other legacy artifacts like modern painting or sculpture. It is denied even the attention granted to other ubiquitous categories such as industrial design, furniture, fashion, and photography.

"Many of the automobiles produced in the 20th century deserve to be looked at in the way an art historian looks at pieces of art," says Miles Collier, founder of the REVS Institute in Naples, Florida, which houses a museum of more than 100 significant cars and has a research facility dedicated to the automobile and our relationship with it. "They are important in and of themselves. They are not just a manifestation of cultural practice."

This lack of serious inquiry is reflective of a tendency to see the car as a quotidian object, one that is functional as a means of transportation with just enough design and features to regularly convince the public it needs them. The tendency for automotive histories—the anecdotes connected to a vehicle's creation, use, and provenance—to acquire tangled elements of obfuscation and embellishment contributes to this deficit.

"I think the very nature of car stories as an art form requires a certain degree of exaggeration to make them totally charming," says

Previous: Century-old National race cars. *Photo by James Lipman*

Opposite: 12-cylinder engine, 1971 Porsche 917K. *Photo by Matt Tierney*

Collier. "But it depends on what kind of car story we're talking about. If we're sitting over beers, it ought to be like the analogy of a fish story. If we're talking about trying to get to the bottom of a historic narrative, then you're dealing with something else."

Mike Kunz, who for 15 years has run the Mercedes-Benz Classic Center—a subsidiary of Mercedes-Benz North America dedicated to researching, preserving, restoring, and buying and selling significant cars from the marque's 133-year heritage—has a similar time-worn take. "Everyone has a different version of the truth," he says, chuckling. "We've had so many cases where a car is described in a certain way, and I often wonder if it's because people don't have the same eyes that we have, or if they're delusional, or just overly optimistic."

Intentional or ambiguously unintentional, this tale telling accretes over a vehicle's life, passing from owner to owner like a game of Telephone, with details becoming increasingly distorted or obtuse, often making the car seem more obscure or valuable.

"There are definitely people who think they have something really important, and they very much believe that, and it's no fault of their own. It was perhaps conveyed to them by somebody else, or it was a fact pattern surrounding the car that made it sort of, could be possible," says Mark Gessler, former director of the Historic Vehicle Association (HVA), a nonprofit partnered with the U.S. Department of the Interior and the Library of Congress to create the National Historic Vehicle Register, similar to the National Register of Historic Places, but for important vehicles in American heritage. "And then there's material fraud," Gessler says. "It's unfortunately much like the art world or any other collectible. There will always be some profit to be made out of forgery. It exists at all levels of the market, from a $2000 car to a $20 million car."

To ascertain the value or relevance of a vehicle—for a buyer or seller, or for it to be considered for inclusion in an exclusive concours or museum exhibit—it is important to uncover a car's truth. This can be accomplished in various ways, and to varying degrees, often dependent on the potential price and/or noteworthiness of the vehicle.

"The higher the value of the car, the higher the burden of proof—the knowledge, the documentation—is required," says Colin Comer, a highly trusted automotive authenticator and author who runs Colin's Classic Automobiles in Milwaukee, Wisconsin, and is the Marketplace director for Hagerty. "If it's a $20,000 car and everything seems to be okay with the paperwork, then you're okay with it quacking like a duck and walking like a duck. But if it's a $50 million car, then you really have a high standard to meet."

This standard is particularly high when the vehicle's provenance is being endorsed officially by an automotive brand. Some marques subcontract this process to licensees, like Pontiac Historic Services for Pontiacs, or Marti Reports for Fords. Others, like Ferrari (Ferrari Classiche) or Lamborghini (PoloStorica), have moved this practice in house, where it has become a profit center. These certifying bodies have manufacturing databases at their disposal, something often unavailable to a lay investigator. This is particularly relevant in the upper echelons of the market, where customization, and thus deviations from the norm, are more common.

"I always say you can never speak in absolutes, because there are exceptions, especially with premium cars because they were often built for special people," says Kunz. "If you're the prince of the Netherlands, and you say, in 1958, that you want a 300SL roadster with Rudge wheels, and they only made them in 1957, you're going to get your Rudge wheels, and your car won't be consistent with the rest of the production run. But we have excellent records from the factory, and we can find the original build sheet in our archives so we know it's accurate."

Standards can be higher still when one is charged with certifying the vehicular heritage of an entire nation, as is the HVA. Thus far, the organization has placed its imprimatur on two dozen remarkable vehicles, from an original Myers Manx dune buggy, to the first Indianapolis 500–winning race car, to a classic lowrider. These cars have impeccable and well-documented pedigrees and amazing originality. But for entrée into this elite grouping, they must be able to communicate a unique four-pronged connection to our vehicular history: being a part of a relevant event; providing a link with a notable person; demonstrating distinctive engineering or design features; and being extremely rare, impeccably preserved, or thoughtfully restored.

"There is always some piece of paper, some evidentiary fact, that links a particular vehicle with its past. Usually, when you don't have that, it's a bunch of conjecture," says Gessler of the daunting task of authentication, which can take years for one vehicle. "It's something about the fact pattern and the material truth of the artifact. So it has to be authentic and have a direct and demonstrable link to the past."

To uncover this truth, automotive archaeologists have developed all manner of tools, some of them straightforward, some of them a bit more devious, some of them dependent on good fortune. Fans of television programs like *CSI* will find overlap. "It's detective work, plain and simple," says Comer. "I mean, it's tracking things down."

This attempt at verification often begins with locating some part of a paper trail, actual or virtual, to connect a vehicle with its germane context. This could mean a Google title search, or a physical search through registration records in the locale in which the car was first sold. From there, it's best to find people who owned or knew the car, or to locate their descendants. "Sometimes you need to find the oldest gas station in town and talk to the guy who owns it and ask, 'Do you remember a kid with a Camaro with an aluminum engine?'" says Comer.

From there, next steps might include paying for an online search and receiving the address of everyone in the country who shares the potential owner's name, then writing them all a letter and asking if they're the Craig Gould who once owned a turquoise 1963 Avanti. "You'd be surprised how often that works," says Comer. Or it might include attempting, visually, to document a car's history. "If you think a car raced at Road America in 1958, you can call the *Sheboygan County Press* to see if it has any pictures on file from that race, and see if there's a picture of the car, or look at race results," Comer suggests.

Sometimes these are dead ends, or inconclusive, and the only option is to get into the car itself to look for evidence of its provenance. For

1954 Mercedes-Benz 300SL Gullwing. *Photo by Matt Tierney*

Early morning at the 2017 Goodwood Revival. *Photo by Amy Shore*

146

example, a classic Mercedes 300SL Gullwing had various stampings applied at the factory, and their particular sequence, application, and location is a kind of complex hieroglyphic that is subject to definitive interpretation by those fluent in the language.

"Some are numbered in relation to one another, and some are numbered not in any relation to the car," says Kunz. "Sometimes when people try to fake things, they'll put numbers on components that shouldn't be numbered, or they'll change the number or the font or the manner in which the number has been applied." Kunz has even seen cases where a number has been stamped into the frame, a task that requires a good deal of force and a sledgehammer. If the imprint is perfectly clean and appears without any denting, this raises suspicion as well.

Intriguingly, these numerological interrogations can be confounded by even the standard practice of seeking out "numbers matching" cars—vehicles with their factory installed and stamped components still in place. "Part of the problem we have," Kunz says, "is that back in the '50s and '60s, if you replaced an engine through the factory, the company received instructions to transfer the number."

Sometimes authentication can only occur with dismantling a part of the vehicle. "What I need you to do is remove the rear fender of the car" was the frightening advice Mark Gessler gave to the new owner of a seven-figure '30s Alfa Romeo purchased at auction. "That's where the serial number is," Gessler says.

These investigations don't always work out as planned. In a major disappointment to the gentleman who had paid more than $1 million for the Italian race car, the number found beneath the back wing was seemingly correct for the model but was revealed to be stamped through the paint. This meant it was added after the car had been restored, and thus a forgery. "When we took off that paint, there was another serial number under there. It was for an Alfa Romeo, but a much less valuable Alfa Romeo," Gessler says.

On occasion, when prising apart a valuable car with a mysterious provenance, luck will prevail. A chip of paint flaked from the edge of a wheel connected a restored and maroon-repainted '53 Allard J2X to its origin as a yellow car used in the melodrama *Written on the Wind* starring Rock Hudson and Lauren Bacall. A bit of interior trim removed from a restored sports car might reveal a clue to a past owner.

"I didn't really know the history of a certain Ferrari, but when I pulled off the driver's side door panel, I found a "For Sale" sign that had fallen in there, with a phone number," says Comer. He was able to trace the number to a person who confirmed having owned the car, as well as providing the name of the person from whom he'd purchased it. "Then, all of a sudden, the floodgates opened. You get one owner, then the second, then the next," says Comer.

Provenance can even be proved by touch. Comer often reunites suspected prior owners with cars he is attempting to authenticate to see if they remember obscure quirks or details. "I'll ask, 'Is this your old car?' and they'll put their hand under the seat and go, 'Oh, yeah. This is where my kid ripped the leather when he was 12,'" Comer says. "If they sign an affidavit, that's good enough for me."

As it turns out, "good enough" is a relative term for these archaeologists. Once they're on the hunt, it can often be difficult for them to figure out when to stop. "I'm not a drug addict, but I imagine it's kind of like heroin. Like, *Oh, man, I just need some more,*" Comer says. "You get into it. It's like watching a detective movie and stopping in the middle. You really need to know the whole story."

This monomaniacal quest can lead beyond an object's provenance. It can facilitate the discovery of something thought to be lost to history. As one develops prominence as a knowledgeable researcher, an owner or an heir with suspicions that something in their possession is exceptional will reach out. "You get a reputation, and things start coming to you," Gessler says. This is not always welcome, or invited. With all the information available online, and the lack of context, owners often believe they have something special. "With so many years of auctions on TV, and the internet," Comer says, "everybody thinks his or her car is worth millions of dollars."

But the trail can lead to a true revelation. Comer relates stories of a previously lost Boss 429 Mustang and a souped-up, first-generation

Ford Bronco prototype, of a previously lost alloy-bodied Ferrari 275 and a big-block Shelby Cobra that subsequently sold for more than $1 million each. "I don't think everything has been found. That's the funny part," he says. "Even with all the news and information, these cars are still out there."

Since they're hidden away for extended periods of time, "barn finds" frequently get lauded as a needed addition to the historical record. But according to experts, just because a vehicle has reappeared doesn't necessarily make it important. "Many barn finds are abused pieces of junk that somebody put away because it wouldn't run anymore. It was stuck in the back of the barn because it broke," says Miles Collier of the REVS Institute. "The best historic cars are those that have been notoriously in the public eye for years and are not restored and have been used responsibly and sympathetically by their owners."

This interest in the historic preservation of exemplary vehicles is one mission of the REVS Institute and the HVA. Together, these organizations have been at the forefront of automotive research and valuation in campaigning for the relevance of not just a vehicle's mechanical or visual accuracy—the existence of matching numbers on the engine and transmission and chassis, the proper factory color in its glossy exterior paint—but also its life as an object and the story that tells.

Much of the emphasis in the collectible-car hobby falls on "condition," based mainly on a vehicle's appearance and adherence to basic taxonomic strictures. "Condition is often an economic equation," Gessler says. "If you want to move a car up from condition #3 to condition #1, you add money and restore it." But the preservation of a vehicle's history is something intrinsic and cumulative, something that can't be added. It can only be erased through insensitive restoration. There is a shift afoot in the hobby that emphasizes the profound value of unrestored, original-condition vehicles. This follows market and collector trends in other categories of artifacts such as furniture or firearms in which the most valued examples are those that retain their history.

"As Americans, the automobile has affected virtually every aspect of our lives. Yet we have few institutions ensuring that truly historic arti-

1963 Chevrolet Corvette Grand Sport.
Photo by Matt Tierney

facts are preserved in perpetuity for the next 500 years," says Gessler. "When we think of those kinds of time lines, you can understand more fully how these artifacts are lost and how, once they're lost, they can't be found."

Collier takes this argument into an even more philosophical realm. He speaks of the differences between researching a car's forensics—the build sheets and sales documentation that are often the gold standard of current archaeological explorations—and examining what he calls its poetics. "This is all the mushy stuff you can't categorize. When these people painted this car, did they have a lot of runs in the chassis paint? Did they get the panel gaps perfect, which they generally didn't?" Collier asks. "Everybody today gets the forensics pretty right, but not that many people get the poetics right."

This is why it is so important to the REVS Institute and the HVA, in their campaign to recognize the validity of the car as a transformative artistic artifact, that unrestored or sympathetically restored cars be maintained as such. Without them, there is a fear that the deeper meaning of the specific object, its historical and cultural significance over time, as well as what it represents as an outstanding signifier of a larger set of objects, is lost. This is why we preserve the Giotto chapel in Padua, or Machu Picchu in Peru, instead of renovating them and creating new simulacra. "You want to be respectful of any completely original artifact because that's the reference artifact that tells you about the world," Collier says. "That's why nobody looks at a photograph of a restored car for reference in working with original artifacts."

Collier and Gessler are avid supporters of the field of automotive archaeology. They are concerned—as are field researchers in other categories of artifact—with not only making historical discoveries but also how best to judge, maintain, and display these finds, our vehicular heritage. One of the goals is to better align automotive preservation with current standards in the maintenance of other relevant artifacts.

"We have this bizarre culture where we go out and show our cars in the bright sun and have them judged against others," Gessler says. "We don't do this with rifles, or tall clocks, or anything else."

There is even discussion that certain well-documented, original vehicles should be taken seriously as works of art, like an unrestored Chippendale highboy, or a Frank Lloyd Wright house, or a Saarinen tea urn. Despite their original functionality, these vehicles should be preserved permanently, perhaps in a public collection, shown and exercised as needed, but not recklessly.

"You don't want the only totally original Lightweight E-type to be owned by some guy who's going to drive the snot out of it at Goodwood. There are plenty of other Lightweight E-types you can drive. They've been repainted, redone, and so on. So you are the steward of a very rare, important, miraculous artifact, and you should treat it accordingly," Gessler says. "It's like having a van Gogh on your wall. Don't throw darts at it!"

"You are the steward of a very rare, important, miraculous artifact, and you should treat it accordingly."

MARK GESSLER, HVA

2017 Goodwood Revival. *Photo by Amy Shore*

11/HUMOR

CARS ARE NOT FUNNY. They are occasionally funny-looking or funny-acting, but that's usually a result of lapses in design or engineering. Mistakes. These are not necessarily desirable in a device that is the second-most-expensive purchase most people will ever make, can accelerate to triple-digit speeds, and can carry one's entire family. So, for example, when Buckminster Fuller's suppository-shaped and safety-touted Dymaxion car rolled over during one of its first demonstrations at the Chicago World's Fair in 1933 and killed its driver, it wasn't exactly cause for guffaws.

"Good comedy is the tension between what is supposed to happen and what's really happening," says John Krewson, comedy writer, editor-at-large for famed humor publication *The Onion,* and contributor to automotive outlets including *Popular Mechanics* and *Road & Track.* "With a car, what you want to happen is what is supposed to happen every single time. I mean, even the most eccentric car person wants a car to be reliable, to start every time. It's almost bad luck to joke about your car."

This poses a conflict for people who desire to wring laughter from the automobile, professionally. "Car's *aren't* funny. That's kind of the problem, isn't it?" says Richard Porter, who has worked as an automotive writer for the past 20 years, much of it as script supervisor on the BBC's wildly popular and humorous automotive television show, *Top Gear,* and its Amazon successor, *The Grand Tour.* "Fortunately, it wasn't like we sat down and went, 'Hey, let's do a comedy car show.' If we had, I think we'd have probably had a real crisis of confidence."

Cars can definitely be fun, a trait that places them somewhere on the humor spectrum in the same way a donkey sits somewhere on the horse spectrum. Cars can even cause a physiological effect on the human limbic system that mimics our response to humor. "One of my first drives in an exotic car was in the early Nineties in David Letterman's Ferrari Dino," says TV comedy writer Spike Feresten, who has penned scripts and skits for David Letterman, *Saturday Night Live, The Simpsons,* and *Seinfeld* and has hosted his own humorous automotive program, *Car Matchmaker with Spike Feresten.* "Dave said to me, 'This is an Italian car. And you're going to drive it. And when you get to third gear, you're going to be laughing.' I drove off and thought maybe Dave's drunk or maybe he's getting senile. I took the car out to Ocean Park, and I got on it. And by God, by third gear, I was cracking up."

This eruption of laughter seems to be based in part on intangibles related to the unexpected, which is, again, on the humor spectrum. "I think it has something to do with motion, noise, and violence," says Jay Lamm, one of the founders of the 24 Hours of Lemons clunker race, an event that takes a sense of humor so seriously, it's inscribed in its official rules. "But it's mostly the absurdity of the fact that you can slightly alter the position of your foot and have this huge impact on the universe around you. That's inherently amusing on some basic level."

This proves that cars are entertaining, a fact in which we can all revel. "Sure, cars can make people happy," says Krewson. "But being happy and being in comedy are not the same thing, as any comedian will tell you."

Luckily for folks toiling in the trenches of automotive humor, cars—like cult classic movies including *The Room* and *Plan 9 from Outer Space*—can occasionally be so bad they're good. This is often based on their inability to perform the very functions for which they were designed. "Almost any Italian or French automobile from about the mid-Fifties through the early Eighties can be funny in just how bad they are at what they do," says Lamm, adding the proviso that he has owned many Italian cars. "The ways in which they fail and disappoint are so highly predictable and so avoidable. Take the Renault Dauphine. I'm pretty sure that from the day those cars were brand-new, as they were rolling off the line, unionized French autoworkers were pissing themselves because it is such a ridiculous car."

Of course, the intrinsic horribleness of a vehicle, and the humor inherent in this, might not be universal. Recognizing this can make it a bit more difficult to find it amusing. "The Trabant is funny. Everyone laughs at it," says Krewson of the wheezy twin-stroke Iron Curtain transport with body panels made of cotton-reinforced resin. "But that's all the people in Eastern Europe had to drive for decades. That car is a symbol of a totalitarian government completely siphoning the will to live out of a populous." Rim shot!

Cars can take a step up the humor taxonomy when they are contextualized. A clown car is funny (well, it's *supposed* to be funny) because it is tiny and filled with a zillion cumbersomely outfitted clowns. A VW Beetle is funny if it's in a race with anything faster than a sleeping baby because it is painfully slow. "I drove a military-spec Humvee to my kids' elementary school for the last day," says Feresten. "I knew their friends would think it was really funny to see them getting out of the valet line in a giant army truck. And they did think it was funny. They thought it was hilarious."

The world of automotive humor is rescued, and provided with endless source material, by the antithesis of humor: the lethal self-seriousness with which the car industry takes itself. Because automakers' core goal is to sell vehicles, and because they are forced to revise these cars constantly to keep them compelling, they often enter into a hyperbolic feedback loop in which they are forced to make borderline or flagrantly specious claims delivered with the earnest solemnity of a mortician.

"It's probably easy to get swept along by the idea that it's all very serious and important. The importance is almost the funniest thing," says Porter, "this sense that 'we've revised all the exterior trim packages for the 2019 model year.' As if they're curing cancer. Or they say things like, 'This car is a game changer.' Well, no. Penicillin was a game changer. But I'm afraid to say, as marvelous as it probably is, this is just some new BMW."

Vintage Volkswagen Beetle. *Photo by Ben Woodworth*

1960 Chevrolet Corvair. *Photo by Richard Pardon*

This self-importance can extend to other areas of the car hobby, such as racing. "Motorsports isn't inherently funny, but because it's serious, lots of intelligent people end up fretting over something as meaningless as hundredths of a second," says Porter. "If you think about that, it's ridiculous. That's no way for adults to spend their time." Porter wrote a joke about a race car driver bragging that he'd just shaved two-tenths of a second off the lap record at the track. In response, his wife said, "Great, what's he going to do with it? Have a quick fart?"

Nowhere is this self-seriousness on display more flagrantly than at high-end automotive concours like Pebble Beach in northern California and Villa d'Este in northern Italy. At these events, extremely wealthy car collectors, for whom time is money, expend great quantities of time fretting and battling with one another about fastidious details of a classic vehicle's restoration. With the cars valued in the seven- or eight-figure range, it becomes increasingly difficult to see how a hand-crafted vintage leather strap on the boot of a wicker-bodied Rolls-Royce is funny. The moment when the 250GT California crashes out of the house in *Ferris Bueller's Day Off* is funny because it didn't happen, and because it didn't happen to your car.

But poking a hole in these po-faced tendencies is at the root of much automotive humor. The car is a celebratory object, and it best conveys its promise when it is used how it is meant: as a vehicle to deliver joy.

Fortunately, there has been something of a countervailing shift in recent years toward automobile companies and vehicular events taking themselves a bit less seriously. Proclamations from product planners or chief executives might not be any less embellished, but at least some manufacturers—from Kia to VW to BMW—now routinely attempt to insert humor into their consumer communications and advertising. If these aren't funny enough, Richard Porter's personal automotive website, Sniff Petrol, creates some of the most hysterical (fake) car ads you will ever see.

In addition, a new breed of automotive events has emerged, one that reveres and celebrates the automobile but does so imbued with a sense of humor. Jay Lamm's 24 Hours of Lemons races might have kicked off this concept. By placing a $500 maximum on the price of a car that must complete a grueling endurance race, the event naturally self-selects a field of vehicles that are shoddy, but knowingly so. By encouraging costumes for participants and vehicles, Lemons creates an outlet for obvious and not-so-obvious referential jokes—a Chevy Lumina minivan fashioned into a giant DustBuster, a Mercury Villager minivan with a Village People livery. By rewarding the most interesting and inventive team ideas, it encourages participants to become almost Dadaist in their approach.

"Lemons reflects this glorious impulse toward joy," says Krewson. "It admits that cars are disposable goods. We love them, but they're ultimately going to get used up. So it says, let's use them up in a way that entertains us as much as possible and not take ourselves too seriously doing it. That is the purest expression of humor."

Lemons has also spawned a spin-off concours scene of its own, the Concours d'Lemons, which features oddball, unloved, underappreciated, or just plain awful vehicles, often from orphan or underrepresented marques, often from the "Malaise Era" of the Seventies and Eighties, when build quality and performance were at their nadir and baroque features like landau bars and button-tufted velour were at their pinnacle. These vehicles are loved and lauded on-site and off-, just like vehicles in a "real" concours. The affection is at once sincere and knowing. If it were simply ironic, it would be tedious, but there is genuine affection. In honoring the weirdness, it tips into a perverse hilarity.

The joy inherent in Lemons has now bled out to help found other sly and costumed automotive events like Hagerty's Festival of the Unexceptional in the U.K., which honors a similar era of British and European cars, and RADwood, which celebrates cars of the Eighties and Nineties. Even though automotive-comedy experts respect these new destinations, there are other long extant and homegrown subcultures they feel express an even more interesting approach to the locus of vehicular hilarity.

"Many American customizers have a great sense of humor, like George Barris," Krewson says of the California wizard who created the Batmobile, KITT, Black Beauty, the Munster Koach, and the Beverly

Hillbillies Jalopy. "It's broad comedy, but it's still comedy. *Airplane!* is still a funny movie even though it's broad comedy."

Krewson reserves special affection for donk culture, the literal elevating of unloved Nineties domestic sedans via lift kits, giant wheels, and custom paint jobs. "Donk culture gets humor," he says. "It understands that this is the ultimate clown-ass end of the logical, the reductio ad absurdum of American car culture. Huge wheels. Absurd trim and lighting. It often even has corporatelike paint jobs for no reason. I've seen a UPS-themed donk. It's aping NASCAR culture and making fun of it. This is the closest to edgy comedy that car culture comes—the apex of everything I love taken too far. A donk is an all-frosting cake."

The existence of this much automotive joy, celebration, and subversion on any local street corner raises an important issue about our notion of vehicular enjoyment. "The question is maybe not 'why are certain events fun?'" says Lamm. "The question is 'why aren't they *all* fun?' Because nobody *needs* to be doing something with cars. If the car is a device for transportation, you buy a $900 Camry and you're way ahead of the curve. Everything else is for fun and gratification."

One of the ways to make cars more humorous is, perhaps, to sideline the car in the attempt. As in our discussion of the recent changes in the role of the car in automotive communities, there is a movement in automotive comedic enterprises to make the car the vehicle for amusement, as opposed to its object.

On *Top Gear* and *The Grand Tour*, Porter works hard to make sure the automotive content takes a—*ahem*—back seat to the camaraderie among presenters Jeremy Clarkson, James May, and Richard Hammond. "The cars are the starting point and the platform, and they *can* be very funny," Porter says of the writing for the show. "But they are funniest when the guys are talking about one another and to one another, and not necessarily about the cars themselves."

This is even truer of other humorous car-themed series that seem to have garnered *Top Gear*–like crossover success, including Jerry Seinfeld's *Comedians in Cars Getting Coffee* or James Corden's *Carpool Karaoke*. These shows work as humor because, according to Lamm, "the cars are utterly incidental." The performance—whether it be banter between celebrities and comedians in classic cars, or musical performances between a host and famous musicians in posh Range Rovers—occurs inside the car, but it is not about the car.

Of course, like *Top Gear* and *The Grand Tour,* these programs wouldn't work without the car as a clever hook. "There's still something in the car thing," says Porter. "The car is the right prop for those three guys. It's a prop they're comfortable with. If a trio of whimsical chefs had a show and you did an episode where they didn't cook anything or eat anything but were just riding horses around you'd go, 'Oh, come off it. Get back to what you do best.'"

12/ THE SOCIAL NETWORK

A PADDOCK OF JUMPSUITED TEAMMATES filling tires with precise quantities of air. A group of greasy hot rodders wrenching on a V-8 in the baking desert sun. A cluster of tweed-capped British-roadster owners colonizing a state-park picnic area after a drizzly drive. A cravated steward of an Italian exotic buffing his pride on an exclusive golf green. The racers, the hot rodders, the marque clubbers, and the concours attendees have long formed the core of our notion of car communities. Collections of people organized around the automobile.

Camaraderie is a keen goal of such groups, along with their value as a locus to dork out ad infinitum on the arcane automotive bunkum about which one's other friends and family members might have become bored, or borderline murderous. The car itself is the nucleus around which activity is oriented, as well as the qualifying entity that grants entrée. It is, literally and figuratively, "the thing."

"Our parents' generation was more object oriented," says Zac Moseley, the 40-year-old codirector of Classic Car Club Manhattan, a popular fractional-car-ownership club and clubhouse in New York City. "Their sense of accomplishment was finally going out and buying that Corvette. Rolling it out in the driveway on the weekend, washing it while their neighbors were driving by."

This position of primacy imbues the automobile with a kind of reverence—for its glories of design and engineering, for its intrinsic capabilities, for its monetary value. "The way I was raised, I was told, 'You have to respect this valuable, expensive, historically important object,'" says Jay Lamm, the 53-year-old founder of the deliciously viral 24 Hours of Lemons clunker-car racing series.

Checking tire pressure in the Goodwood paddock.
Photo by Amy Shore

Groups like Lamm's and Moseley's are often founded on a kind of siloed exclusivity, whether around a particular marque or a form of engagement with the vehicle. People in your club are on the inside, and people who do not adhere to your affection for, say, autocrossing air-cooled, rear-engined sports cars are automatically placed outside your group and often considered heretical.

"The automotive community has always encompassed a bunch of subcultures," Lamm says. "In the past—50 years ago, or even 30 years ago—you were a vintage-car guy, or you were a muscle-car guy, or you were a hot-rod guy, or you were a Pebble Beach guy. I don't think those cultures were particularly tolerant of, or interested in, each other."

But in the contemporary era, this is changing. And it's changing quite rapidly, hopefully for the better and almost certainly out of need.

The most significant shift in current automotive communities involves the role of the central object. The car is no longer the end in and of itself. "I think our generation is less attached to things and more interested in a variety of experiences," says Moseley. "If you want to get out and do something exciting, a car is the way to do that."

Sure, there are impersonal online forums in which nearly anonymous members flame one another about the relative performance superiority of car X against all comers, usually without ever having driven the machine in question. But the most vital, interesting, and fastest-growing car communities are now interpersonal and active. They take the car off its podium, place it squarely back into the living world, and welcome into its wake as broad a range of people as possible.

Lamm may have been one of the progenitors of this new form of organizing when, 12 years ago, he founded the 24 Hours of Lemons, an endurance race for $500 vehicles. The series started in California with a single event but quickly mushroomed. It now boasts an international footprint, dozens of annual races, and a codified subculture of exuberance and irreverence that involves florid curses, outrageous bribes, medieval punishments, and the kind of flamboyant outfitting of cars, drivers, and spectators that wouldn't look out of place at a Brazilian gay-pride parade.

Lamm credits the success of Lemons to two core factors. First, he removed the barriers of fear and shame from vehicular fun. "There's a big group of people," he says, "who always wanted to get on a race-track and go racing, and they were intimidated by the perceived exclusivity and the sense that if they showed up and were not successful, they would be made fun of or looked down on. Lemons has given those people a place to go. Because we don't take ourselves too seriously, that has made it a lot easier for people who've fantasized about it but were intimidated."

Second, Lamm says, he removed the barrier of price. The old saw holds that you make a small fortune in racing by starting with a large one, and it's rooted in truth. By focusing the event on affordable and even disposable vehicles, Lamm eliminated this risk. "It's pretty fun to get a car and go racing with it, particularly when it's not a $100,000 precious thing or a $500,000 precious thing," he adds. "If the worst possible outcome happens, well, it was just a beat-up old BMW, and so it goes."

The success of Lemons and the inclusive joy inherent in its model have spawned all manner of communities organized around similar principles. Chris Stewart, a 39-year-old Chicago creative director in advertising, founded the Gridlife festival at GingerMan Raceway in western Michigan in 2013. He did so out of a desire to break down segmentation in automotive communities, especially for the younger participants.

"I kind of got into cars late," Stewart says. "I didn't even get a license until I was 19, and my path of automotive enthusiasm ultimately went from LED washer nozzles on my 1991 Honda CRX to autocross and the track-day world." Stewart attended local and regional track activities and Porsche Club of America events, but there weren't a lot of organizations that felt welcoming to a young kid in a Honda with clear taillights who wanted to drift and race and listen to electronic dance music. So he invented one.

Gridlife combines a host of seemingly discrete events into one festival with open lapping, drifting, and time attack (single-car timed laps

around the circuit). Car shows take place all weekend. Stewart provides for quality food and beverage services, camping, picnics, and side excursions. Everything is combined with a constant run of headlining hip-hop, electronic, and alternative music acts, as well as a late-night dance club.

Participants and observers usually attend a range of events at each festival, affording overlap among distinct social groups. The various factions are intentionally paddocked together with the aim of fostering mutual understanding. For example, the road racers in BMW M3s are forced into camaraderie with the drifters in Honda S2000s.

The Gridlife festival has gone from a one-off event to a twice-annual, weekend-long experience. Stewart also hosts track days under the brand and has started an emergent lifestyle component. Gridlife continues to grow.

"We are basically building a good time for anyone who's into cars or is a friend of someone who is into cars. We're thinking about the different things those individuals might like," Stewart says, "and then it's about removing boredom. Your day begins at 9:00 in the morning, and then it's 9:00 at night, and you don't know where the time went, because there are so many different bits and pieces, you don't have time to be stagnant."

Tate Morgan, 38, of Portland, Oregon, experienced a similar epiphany prior to founding the Gambler 500 in 2014. Like Lemons, the Gambler uses $500 vehicles as a starting point. But instead of sustaining hours of track abuse, these vehicles are taken on an untimed two-day rally across a routeless, on-and-off-road course bounded only by supplied GPS coordinates. The emphasis is on the experience and the interpersonal connections. Absent the pressure of time, there's no reason not to stop and help your cohorts if, for example, their axle breaks. Bonds and stories form naturally.

"'Fun is greater than rules' has always been our tagline," Morgan says. "We celebrate being vague in our definition of what the event is. Once you get in the car with your buddies, part of the fun is figuring it out along the way. Not everybody has the same experience. Not everyone

A costumed Mazda Miata running a 24 Hours of Lemons race.
Photo by Alfred J. Bautista

Tanner Foust in a modified Volkswagen Passat drift car during a Gridlife event.
Photo by Larry Chen

is going on the same road. I think it's a little bit of the unknown. That, in and of itself, creates new challenges and fun, unexpected things."

The notion of real-life adventure is a core attraction of this new cadre of automotive communities. It's what draws people in initially and what causes them to return with new participants in tow. You might suppose this is a reaction to the homebound virtual world—the internet—that now so dominates our existence. But it seems just as likely to exist *because* of the internet.

In short, the internet is good for car communities. First, it diminishes barriers to exposure and connection with experiences that might potentially move you. Whatever your interest, you can now readily locate other people and organizations who can support and help deepen your love for a given machine or culture. "Anyone who has a hobby in the connected age can find people to share that hobby with," says Southern California's Matt Farah, 36. Since 2006, Farah has created a series of wildly popular YouTube videos under the name *The Smoking Tire*. In addition to spawning a successful podcast, his creative efforts have allowed him to engage with and host pretty much the entire American automotive world.

He notes that the internet provides the capability to feed and maintain those interests virtually, keeping them from flaming out due to lack of fuel. "I'm a big fan of driving rally cars in the snow," Farah says by example. "But I don't have to go to the mountains to keep that interest active all the time. I can experience that digitally"—through YouTube, gaming, social media, forums, the list is virtually endless—"from the beach here in California."

The internet offers ease of dissemination for alluring ideas and content, magnifying the profile and potential participant base for a compelling event or group. It may seem obvious, but the potential for profound exposure can't be overstated. Stewart from Gridlife and Morgan from the Gambler attest that explosive interest in their events could be traced directly to a few viral articles or videos. In the Gambler's first year, 40 cars participated. By 2018, four years later, there were 680.

A cynical person might think this outpouring of attraction is simply the result of people attempting to collect virtual souvenirs—photos posted on social media with the goal of making friends and followers jealous. But it seems to derive from an expansion of viewers' imaginations regarding automotive opportunity. "I think social media and all the imagery give people access to dream bigger and go check out more stuff," says Moseley. "And then they see, through communities like ours, that there are ways to get out and actually do it, instead of just reading about it and seeing it."

Farah agrees. "You don't have to buy a thing. You don't have to have the bigger house. You don't have to have the bigger diamond. You just have to go on the biggest adventure. The internet has really driven the idea of adventuring and expeditioning."

Farah isn't paying lip service to this concept's allure. He's essentially adopted it as a personal mantra. By way of example, he recently discovered off-road sports cars via the internet and has thrown himself deep into the hobby. "I am putting way too much money into a Safari 911 build," he says. A friend and former professional road racer from Georgia, Leh Keen, is currently helping Farah craft an off-road-ready version of an Eighties Porsche 911. Keen has a small business building cars like this, all of which pay homage to Stuttgart's rally history and are currently fashionable.

Since he spends his life exploring automotive subcultures, it isn't surprising that Farah is precisely on trend here. The experience of venturing into the unknown and unexpected is another core allure of today's automotive communities.

The reasons behind this are diverse, and telling. The first is simply that modern road cars have become too good. Forty or even 30 years ago, it was possible to drive down a winding back road in a contemporary sports car and approach the vehicle's limits safely, without undue risk or excessive speeding. But rapid advancements in driveline and chassis technology have resulted in modern sports cars capable of doubling or sometimes tripling a back road's speed limit without so much as flirting with the edge of their ability. Surveys and sales figures indicate that this has helped diminish public interest in new, high-performance road cars, and the change follows logic: It's difficult to get excited about constantly replicable perfection at five-tenths of a machine's potential. Off in the wilderness, or the desert, or the snowpack, the car is forced to overcome more adversity, handicapping it and making it more interesting.

Additionally, the idea of an adventure, especially an uncertain one—like taking a $500 car on, say, a daylong race or a weekend-long overland outing—might serve as an antidote to our all-knowing, constantly connected times.

"I think we go back to technology," Morgan says. "You can pick up your phone and Google just about anything and get a reasonable answer. Stepping out into the woods and not knowing what's around the corner, or if your not-so-reliable rig will make it, force us to handle challenges as they come, without being too concerned about the outcome."

This quest for the unknown in an age of ubiquitous answers inhabits other aspects of emerging car communities. With encyclopedic computing power in our pockets and cumulative decades of obsessing over enthusiast publications and car shows, contemporary car lovers seem to have become slightly exhausted with the familiar canon of significant vehicles: Bearcat, SJ, Gullwing, E-type, GTO, Miura, Testarossa, Veyron.

These vehicles have made the concours rounds for years. We are now looking for what we don't know—not what we do. These new events provide an opportunity to see and celebrate that. The result isn't simply another triumph of irony. It's a celebration of the weird, the odd, the personal, and the specific. It's about admiring imperfection in an age of perfection—the former, of course, being at the root of loving a mechanical object that will inevitably break and break down, and possibly break your heart.

"I always say that an Alfa 8C is a wonderful, incredible, fabulous thing. But I've seen it about 50 times now. I've seen every one of them. I've sat in a few of them. And I just don't need to do it again," says Lamm. "But a guy shows up in a Renault Dauphine with a hot-rod motor, and he's driving that thing all crossed up in an 800-mile-a-day rally? Well, I've never seen that before. That's pretty great." This sentiment flows

1972 Datsun 240Z.
Photo by Will Broadhead

1967 Lamborghini Miura.
Photo by Matt Tierney

over into the means by which cars are utilized in these popular new subcultures. From drifting a convertible pickup, to racing a minivan, to off-roading a Geo Metro, participants focus on lionizing the oddball and celebrating the ingenuity involved in unintended use.

"If you manage to get a stretch limo or an 80-foot articulated city bus through a trail that was made to be occupied by a purpose-built overland rig," Morgan says, "you're definitely cooler than the guy who does it in a Toyota Tacoma or Jeep with bolt-on [off-roading] kits." You're probably also having a better, more memorable time.

This breaking down of barriers—financial, participatory, and among subcultures—is not solely a part of some scheme to make the hobby more inclusive. With commutes increasing in length and impinging on leisure time, with the incontrovertible contribution of tailpipe emissions to climate change, popular opinion on the automobile has started to shift. Many people now consider the car more social problem than triumphant solution. Banding together under the banner of enthusiasm for the machine feels necessary.

"Ours is an audience that is potentially shrinking," Stewart says. "We are too small a niche to have segmentation. We need to find ways to overlap and come together, because we're stronger together."

The explosive growth of communities using the automobile as a tool for unpredictable adventure demonstrates another narrative—one that transcends the moribund or anachronistic. It's the notion that it's possible to embrace change and still be proud. "I'm the last person who's going to preach about millennials not wanting to drive cars," says Morgan. "Who wants to force people into something they don't want to do? Cultures change and shift. If self-driving cars and public transportation and walking or bicycling are trending, I think those are good things."

Exposure is essential in shifting perceptions. These expanding webs of Gamblers and Gridlifers will inevitably include a friend who isn't a gearhead. A few people might scream in fury or beg to get out. But far more are likely to laugh. Cars have that effect on the human limbic system in part because they're uncanny. They do things you don't expect.

Things you're afraid of. Things that delight you. They *move* you, and this kind of incidental movement provides the best opportunity to catalyze people, as Gridlife's Chris Stewart says, "to move from car curious to car engaged."

A longing for the alchemical camaraderie of a cramped passenger cabin. A devotion to the unique joy proffered by the combination of wind, speed, and road—or roadlessness. Being a member of the faithful does not obligate one to proselytize, and it shouldn't require one to disparage emergent alternatives.

Loving an automobile for what it is can feel abstract and unrelatable. Loving a vehicle for what it can do and provide is emotional, universal, and infectious.

"We like to say that if you have a pulse, and you haven't had some horrible experience with cars, you can't walk into our club and not put a smile on your face," says Classic Car Club Manhattan's Moseley. "There are things that happen around cars that excite everybody."

13/MY LAST DRIVE

"THE LAST MEAL" IS A KIND OF CHEF'S PARLOR GAME, an opportunity for cooks, typically over many drinks, to discuss the ideal menu for their final dining experience. It might sound a bit morbid, but it isn't. It's just a thought exercise, an occasion for celebrating, imaginatively and with no holds barred, all that is wonderful about gastronomy—the sense of creativity, the endless and original combinations of obscure ingredients, the progression of courses and pairings. It is about that evanescent quest, the endless hunt, for that alchemical mixture of components, balance, and literal and figurative good taste. It is an opportunity to show off, to show up, to show your stripes.

Likewise, those of us who love cars and driving have created an analogous diversion. If we could plot our "Last Drive," our perfect final time behind the wheel, where would we go? And in what? And with whom?

Each person's answer to this query is as individuated as his or her vehicular (and geographic and companionable) preferences. There is no correct or incorrect response, but there is, of course, endless room for debate. Roadster, boulevardier, grand tourer, pickup? On-road, off-road, on-track, on the moon? Alone, with a loved one, with an enemy, with your god? The vehicle must suit the task, and the task must suit the vehicle and one's needs.

To reflect the diversity and passion of the American driver, we asked a broad group of notable people, in or adjacent to the automotive world, to define their perfect Last Drive. Here are their answers.

BILL WARNER, FOUNDER, AMELIA ISLAND CONCOURS

WHERE I'D GO: It would all depend on where the hearse was going! But if I were still available to drive, I think it would be on the French and Italian rivieras along the Côte d'Azur. It's probably the most beautiful place in the world as you go along the Mediterranean, up and down the hills. And then I'd drive up to Lake Como, and I'd drive around Lake Como and Lake Garda. And then I'd check into the local funeral home.

WHAT I'D DRIVE: My 1971 Porsche 911, which I've owned since '71. It's nimble, it's light, it's pretty, it handles good. I've bumped it up to a 2.7-liter flat-six with about 200 horsepower, so it has plenty of power. If you're going to pull up to the Hôtel de Paris Monte-Carlo in Monaco, you're not going to drive up in a gray Chevelle. And it's better than being in a black Cadillac station wagon.

WHO WOULD JOIN ME: It'd be my wife, Jane. And I think I'd just better leave it at that. Anything else would cause me grief at home. It'd be my wife of 53 years.

BOB LUTZ, RETIRED EXECUTIVE, GM, FORD, CHRYSLER

WHERE I'D GO: I'd pick the Angeles Crest Highway, east of L.A. It's just fantastic. It's fast and it's got lots of sweepers and it goes higher and higher. The road surface is good. The only thing bad about it is the speed limit and the other traffic. But in this fantasy, it's my private road.

WHAT I'D DRIVE: My 1952 Cunningham C4R. It's less than 2000 pounds. It has 400 horsepower out of a Chrysler 331 Hemi. And it handles just right for a road like that. It's extremely agile and flickable, and, because in the Fifties when even racing tires were relatively narrow, you can really hang the tail out on sharp bends. It's probably not as fast as if I had said I'd take my 2010 Corvette ZR1, but I'm sure it would be a far more entertaining drive. More driver involvement, more skill involved, heavier steering. In a less capable chassis, the limit is much closer in.

WHO WOULD JOIN ME: I love my wife, but the answer is nobody. You want maximum enjoyment. You want the thrill of doing it to the best of your and the car's capabilities. If you have anybody with you, those things all kind of deteriorate.

C.J. WILSON, RACE CAR DRIVER, RACE TEAM OWNER, FORMER MAJOR LEAGUE BASEBALL PITCHER

WHERE I'D GO: I'm kind of conflicted. I've had a chance to drive the Targa Florio, I've driven a couple really awesome routes in America, and I've had a chance to drive on every continent except Australia. I drive about 30,000 miles a year, so I'd have to do something I haven't done yet. I think I'd have to do the Dakar rally. It would be grueling, and challenging.

WHAT I'D DRIVE: You have to take one of those big Bowler Rally Raid vehicles. Or a one-off Red Bull car like the Touareg they did. They're like buggies, but realistically, it's a full-on race car.

WHO WOULD JOIN ME: I wouldn't want to take anyone with me if it's the implication that something bad would happen. But if it's both of our last drives, I would take my wife. You need a codriver, navigator. We've gone on a lot of cool road trips together, and there aren't too many other people I'd want to spend 10 or 12 days with in a row. There's not a lot of incentive to pick someone else.

DAN NEIL, AUTOMOTIVE COLUMNIST, THE *WALL STREET JOURNAL*

WHERE I'D GO: I'm going to take the "thanatopsis" approach to this last drive. If I am ever really sick and I'm going to die, I have scoped out this road. It is the road to Kitt Peak National Observatory outside Tucson. It's a lot like Pikes Peak, but with absolutely no guardrails. There are sweepers on this road that look like Le Mans—big, huge, geologically scaled sweepers. So, what I thought was, I'd go off right about there. About 4500 to 5000 feet of elevation.

WHAT I'D DRIVE: My first thought, of course, is the most expensive man-ufacturer's press car I could find: a Mercedes-Maybach G650. But my dream car is a Facel Vega HK500. In my mind's eye, as I leave this earth in a kind of romantic flourish, that's what I'd be driving. But it's more likely to be like a rental from Hertz.

WHO WOULD JOIN ME: No one. This is a solo flight.

Angeles Crest Highway, California.
Photo by Stefan Bogner

Eilean Donan Castle, Scotland.
Photo by Amy Shore

DARIO FRANCHITTI, RETIRED RACE CAR DRIVER

WHERE I'D GO: It would have to be Scotland. I'd probably start off somewhere around Edinburgh, go up through Gleneagles, up to the Loch Tay area, then head up through Glencoe to the west coast, and then follow some of the roads there, just see where the mood took me. The topography has a lot to do with it. There aren't many straight parts. And there's some good undulation. You're going through beautiful valleys and beautiful glens, going alongside lochs, you're going beside the Atlantic Ocean at different times as well. The scenery is constantly changing, and it's somewhere I grew up in a lot of ways.

WHAT I'D DRIVE: I think my Ferrari Daytona Spider. I think it would suit the mood. It's a little softer and has that beautiful noise coming from the carburetor and the V-12 wailing away.

WHO WOULD JOIN ME: I would take my wife because she loves driving there as much as I do. She loves being in the passenger seat. On one of our first dates, I took her up there in my Porsche Carrera GT, and she actually fell asleep. I was not hanging around on that drive. I thought, "Okay, I think she might be a keeper."

DAVID HOBBS, RETIRED RACE CAR DRIVER, RACE COMMENTATOR

WHERE I'D GO: I think I'd like to have one more go at the Amalfi Coast road down to Portofino. It has some heavy memories of younger days racing when I went to Monte Carlo back in the Sixties. And then in the Seventies I raced a Formula 5000 car at Mugello, a race I just happened to win—I thought I'd mention that. We went down there after the race, and it's a particularly spectacular piece of road, just gorgeous, and of course you're going through some wonderful old villages and old areas that have been around for, you know, thousands of years.

WHAT I'D DRIVE: A nice Bentley Azure with the top down. I have a soft spot for Bentleys. They're hideously expensive, unbelievably expensive to run, make no sense at all. But a pale blue Azure, as its name would imply, is a pretty cool car. At my age, a sports car, like a Ferrari, is out, because I can get into them, but I can't get out again, because it's too low. I can get into and out of a Bentley.

WHO WOULD JOIN ME: Well, I'd take my lifelong companion, my wife, Margaret. We've been married nearly 57 years, so I think it'd be only right and proper that I take her. She's my best friend. I think she'd be a very willing companion. She loves Italy, and she loves the history. She'd be very happy to drive down that road.

ED WELBURN, RETIRED GLOBAL HEAD OF GM DESIGN

WHERE I'D GO/WHAT I'D DRIVE/WHO WOULD JOIN ME: As much as I love to drive, I have even more fun washing a car by hand. I learn a lot about a car when I do that. My favorite car to wash is a '63 Corvette Sting Ray. Just give me a bucket of water, a rag, a glass of red wine, and some nice music, and that's more fun than driving the thing.

But when I was head of design at GM, I worked on designing the Beast, the presidential limousine—the first one and the second one. Those were truly special projects. So this last drive would be in the latest Beast down Pennsylvania Avenue with newly elected President Michelle Obama in the back seat.

For me, that is emotional. I can't even sit down when I think about the idea of driving the Beast down Pennsylvania Avenue with President Michelle Obama in the back seat. That's exciting. That's thrilling.

JAY LENO, COMEDIAN, CAR COLLECTOR

WHERE I'D GO: I don't want to go on my last drive, because that means it's going to be my last drive, you know? But if I were going to go, it would probably be a road I enjoy driving on. A road I've been on a million times. There's a place called Angeles Crest Highway. You have 66 miles through the Angeles National Forest. It can be 80 degrees when you get on the road, and there'll be snow when you get to the top. It's like driving in Sicily or the mountains in Switzerland. You go as high as 6000 or 7000 feet. You're up around Mt. Wilson.

WHAT I'D DRIVE: I've got a Duesenberg that I've had for years, a supercharged Murphy convertible with a disappearing top, which is just a fabulous car. It was the epitome of automobile excellence in its day. It was the fastest, most powerful American car ever built up until the

Chrysler letter cars of the Fifties and Sixties. When other cars could barely go 60 miles an hour, Duesenbergs would do 130. It was pretty impressive.

WHO WOULD JOIN ME: If it's my last drive, I guess it'd be my wife. For the most part, I enjoy driving by myself because then I can take more chances without risking anybody else.

JAY WARD, CREATIVE DIRECTOR, PIXAR

WHERE I'D GO: I would like to drive the complete length of Route 66, going down first to L.A. and then all the way to Chicago and back again. Route 66 has a connection to me through the movie *Cars*. But it also has a connection because I'm a Midwest boy. I was born in Kansas City, Missouri. In fact, I went back to Joplin after tornadoes hit there, and we dedicated a portion of Route 66 to the movie *Cars*.

WHAT I'D DRIVE: My 1957 Pontiac Safari wagon—I drive my kids to school in it—pulling a matching 1957 Airstream Caravanner. I've never taken one of my old cars that far. Even if there are breakdowns, there are some really fun stories. I grew up before there were cell phones, and the stuff you went through with old cars breaking down and the people you met along the way who helped you or made it worse, it all adds to the stories we have. Some of the best stories of my life are those times when you really had to go for it and trust things, and you didn't have a phone in your pocket to save you. There's something cool about that.

WHO WOULD JOIN ME: If I could get my '57 Safari with the whole family in it, pulling a vintage Airstream so we could stop wherever we wanted, I think that would be a pretty cool bonding family experience to do. That's a bucket list trip I really want to do with my family.

LAURA SCHWAB, PRESIDENT, ASTON MARTIN THE AMERICAS

WHERE I'D GO: When I was a kid in the late Eighties, I played tennis competitively. Tennis is an individual sport, a sport of competition and travel tournaments. My mom and I would pack up the car at the beginning of the summer, and off we'd go. We would just travel, primarily around the South. We learned how to pump gas together for the first time because she'd never pumped her own fuel. We had all these maps printed out, and I would navigate. We found ourselves going the wrong way on a one-way street in the middle of nowhere to get to these tennis tournaments. If I were going to re-create my favorite drive, it would probably be my mom and I driving from Kentucky to West Virginia, Alabama, Mississippi, and Tennessee for a tournament.

WHAT I'D DRIVE: My mom had this Cadillac Allanté, and she had one of the first cell phones, those big phones that were actually built into the car. We thought that was the perfect car, because what if something happened to us out there on the road together?

WHO WOULD JOIN ME: My mom. I love her. She's like my best friend. I think it would be so much fun to do a trip like that with her again.

MARIO ANDRETTI, RETIRED RACE CAR DRIVER

WHERE I'D GO/WHAT I'D DRIVE: I can't get some things out of my system. If I could have my wish granted now, I would give part of my limbs to drive one of today's Formula 1 cars at Spa. I'd raced one in Belgium, but that was in Zolder because Spa was being reconstructed and shortened, so I missed out on Spa. In any Formula 1 driver's account, Spa is the king. Because of Eau Rouge and places like that, there's something about that track that, for us, has that special value.

WHO WOULD JOIN ME: I would've loved to have my wife with me, but I lost Dee Ann on July 2, 2018.

PATRICK DEMPSEY, ACTOR, PORSCHE RACE CAR DRIVER

WHERE I'D GO: I would like to drive on the autobahn because I wouldn't have to worry about the speed limit. I would drive from Stuttgart to Le Mans. Why? Because that says it all!

WHAT I'D DRIVE: I would drive my 1972 911T. The car has such a great feeling to it. It makes me smile. I would also want to drive a 356. It is really difficult to pick just one!

WHO WOULD JOIN ME: I would bring along my wife, Jill, and my kids. We would have to drive the two cars since there are five of us. My family is very competitive, so we would be racing the entire time.

PETER EGAN, EDITOR-AT-LARGE, *ROAD & TRACK* MAGAZINE

WHERE I'D GO: I've been to northern Canada. I've been above the border a few times in the west, into the Canadian Rockies. But I've never crossed the upper Great Plains in Canada and gone through all those out-in-the-plains cities. I've never seen the northern Canadian Rockies, either. I'd like to start at home in Wisconsin and get up to probably Anchorage or Fairbanks.

WHAT I'D DRIVE: I'd want it to be a motorcycle trip. I was just looking at a Honda Africa Twin. I asked my friend Mark Hoyer, editor-in-chief at *Cycle World,* what he would take if he lived in Wisconsin and wanted to ride across Canada and into Alaska and have something that worked on the road and still wasn't too bad off-road. He said the Africa Twin would be toward the top of his list for the job.

WHO WOULD JOIN ME: I was thinking about a solo excursion because I've never had an open-ended trip. I've done a lot of travel for magazines, but I've always had my own schedule or somebody else's where it's absolutely crucial that we get at least as far as Omaha by tonight, or that kind of thing. So you skip some of the interesting roads sometimes, ride by an interesting car for sale and think, "I'd like to stop and look at that, but I just can't. I have to keep rolling." So I'm inclined to do a solo, a very long solo motorcycle trip with no end in sight. You know, sort of a general time, a general month where I might be back.

RALPH GILLES, HEAD OF DESIGN, FIAT CHRYSLER AUTOMOBILES

WHERE I'D GO: I love the rally, the long-form rally format, like the Targas. I've done Newfoundland. I've done the Mille Miglia in Italy. The Targa Tasmania is one race I would love to do. South of Australia there's an island called Tasmania. They take over practically the whole island. Crisscross it over a four-or-five-day period. The vistas, the speed, the fact that the roads are shut down and you can drive as fast as you can. The location is amazing, the beauty, and the fact that it's something I've never done.

WHAT I'D DRIVE: I would take an amazing car like a Viper. The Viper means so much to me as an enthusiast. It's kind of the reason I'm at the company—at least, it sparked my interest to come work here. The Viper is an amazing machine. I've been racing them almost 18 years now, and they're never boring. There's always a new dimension the Viper reveals, if you keep asking more of it.

WHO WOULD JOIN ME: Probably my wife. She's always been a great copilot. She'd scream, but she'd enjoy it.

RICHARD RAWLINGS, STAR OF FAST N' LOUD, OWNER GAS MONKEY GARAGE/BAR N' GRILL

WHERE I'D GO: I really want to run Peking to Paris on the old route. You know, they first started it in 1907. You go through something like 14 countries and every single climate imaginable, from frozen tundra to scorched desert, in and out of Mongolia, Russia. It's a pretty crazy trip. I think they're doing it again in 2020, but I'm hoping that's not my last drive.

WHAT I'D DRIVE: A Thomas Flyer won a version of that race, from New York to Paris, in 1908. I actually just finished refurbishing a 1937 Indy car Shafer 8—it's a Buick straight-eight—and that's what I have in mind for that race, taking my 1937 Indy car and doing it in an open-top roadster because that's what the 1908 Thomas Flyer was. You're out there on your own. There are spots where there's nothing. You have to make do with whatever you find and have in and on the car.

WHO WOULD JOIN ME: If my dad hadn't succumbed to Alzheimer's, I would definitely have taken him. But I think this would probably be a trip I'd want to do with my best friend, Dennis Collins. Between the two of us, we could probably figure out any trouble we got ourselves into. When we're in an unpronounceable town's jail, somehow we'll figure out how to get out.

EPILOGUE

HERE'S HOW I KNOW THE FUTURE IS BRIGHT for people like us who drive cars, talk about cars, dream about cars, collect cars, swap cars, race cars, and tinker with cars.

After high school, my daughter—a Midwest kid who got her driver's license as soon as she was eligible, like generations of Midwest kids before her—attended an art school in New York City, where driving isn't the rite of passage it is elsewhere. On visits, I would gently tease her New York friends about what they were missing by not learning to drive. Like many in their generation, they hadn't yet bothered to get licensed because, well, why would they? They got around on subways and in taxis and Ubers and clearly didn't get what the big deal was about owning a car, much less driving one.

"You have to learn to drive," I'd say. "Don't you want to go fast? Don't you want to feel the wind in your hair as you drive down the road in a convertible? Don't you want to…?"

Usually, they'd politely laugh, the way you do with your friend's dad, and we'd move on to another topic. One time, though, I went a step further and said, "I have an idea for you. How about if I set the three of you up with a cool classic car and you drive coast to coast this summer? It'll be an adventure."

They looked at one another, giggled, and said, "Sure!"

When the summer of 2017 arrived, I arranged a red '67 Camaro (it was the 50th anniversary of Chevy's pony car, after all). The three of them chose a route across the country—the exact opposite of what I'd recommended, of course. I urged them to take the cooler, less congested northern route. They preferred a southern course, despite the fact they were going to be driving a car with a black vinyl interior and no air conditioning during the peak of summer. Kids, right?

McKeel and his
1971 Ford Bronco in
northern Michigan.
*Photo by Gabe
Augustine*

After showing them how to check the oil, change a tire, and so forth, off they went—three young women, one a somewhat experienced driver and two newly licensed—driving 3000 miles without parental supervision from the Brooklyn Bridge toward freedom, adventure, and the Golden Gate Bridge. It was like the Dr. Seuss book come to life: *Oh, the places you'll go!*

Yes, there were breakdowns. Yes, there were calls for roadside assistance. Yes, it was a lot of driving for people not used to it. And yes, it was hot as blazes. But they did it. They completed the classic, coast-to-coast, everyone-should-do-this-once-in-a-lifetime all-American road trip in a cool old car without Bluetooth, GPS, air conditioning, or USB ports.

When I met them in San Francisco, they were beaming ear to ear.

"So are you going to own cars someday?" I asked them.

"Oh, yeah!" they gushed. They were going to save their money, buy a cool car, go on more adventures, etc., etc. I expected that answer. What I didn't expect was their answer to my next question about what surprised them most along their journey.

As one, they said, "Arkansas."

Arkansas?

"Yeah, Arkansas. It was just really beautiful."

Isn't that cool? These are college kids who would have never, not in a million years, visited Arkansas if it weren't for their road trip. And now it's a part of their palette of experiences, as is the road trip, from the colorful bugs smashed on the windshield to the wonderful people they met along the way. No one can take that away from them. All those memories are theirs to keep.

That's the power and value of driving. It's also why I chuckle when people tell me that autonomous technology is going to be the death of cars and driving as we know them.

That simply won't happen. Mass-produced automobiles have been with us since 1908, when the first Model T rolled out of a Ford factory. Even after 110 years, though, the car hasn't managed to kill off our interest in the horse or the simple act of walking to get from one place to another. People still love horses. Horses, in fact, are a $122 billion industry in the U.S. People still like walking, too. The same can be said of other things. Despite digital music, people still dig the sound of vinyl records. Despite Kindles, we still read books made of paper, ink, and glue. Microbreweries abound, and yet home brewing continues to be a "thing." Keeping chickens for the eggs is also popular, even though you can get them cheaper and easier at the store.

Automobiles will be no different. People will always love cars for the simple reason that cars and driving—like everything listed above—make us happy.

For instance, as a part of my job, I give dozens of speeches a year all over North America and around the world. At some of these speeches, I quiz the audience about whether they remember the first time they wobbled away from their parents on a bicycle.

"Remember that feeling?" I ask. "That freedom? That fantastic 'I did it!' exhilaration?"

From their faces it's clear just about everybody does.

"Or how about that first time you took a road trip with friends—remember how great that felt?" Again, eyes light up, and I can almost hear the crackle of feel-good memory synapses firing all over the room.

I could also ask: How about that time you found some killer S-turns on a drive out in the country? How about when you intentionally took that dirt two-track, just to see where it ended? Or the time you rented a limo for the prom for you and a dozen friends? Or the time—full of the pride of youth—you detailed every speck of your old jalopy because she or he was going to be riding in it for the first time and you wanted to make a good impression? Who can't, decades later, immediately recall every last detail about his or her first car? Or favorite car? Or worst car? Who hasn't, at least once, named a car?

It's amazing when you think about it. So many moments and memories in our lives include our cars that there's no way we'll ever give them up. Cars and driving will endure because we love them. It's as simple as that. Technology can't kill love. Truth is, technology is not always a zero sum game. It is not always Godzilla, an inevitable, undeniable force that wipes out everything in its path.

I suspect there's a middle ground, especially when it comes to cars. Look, there's little doubt that autonomous vehicles (AVs) will be fantastic for the human race, whenever they reach scale. And that day is a lot farther off than most forecasters will tell you for a host of reasons—manufacturing realities, product costs, safety concerns, infrastructure, and so on. Every year in the U.S., more than 30,000 people die in traffic accidents. AVs should dramatically lower that number. And since we are a commuting society at this point, AVs will also give us back more of our lives, saving us a billion hours every day, according to one estimate.

You know what some of us will choose to do with that time? We'll use it to drive cool cars in fun locations, far outside cities. There's nothing fun about driving in, say, Manhattan. Cities will be the main beneficiaries of autonomy, leaving the rest of the world's rural highways and byways for those of us who enjoy a steering wheel in our hands.

Here's the reality: At its worst, technology steals our attention, our presentness, and our humanity. A good example is smartphones. They have their uses, to be sure, but the cost of staring constantly at a screen is an incremental decline in our interest in interacting with the world around us, including the people in it. The young are especially impacted. "Today's teenagers go out less and are less likely to hold a job," author Malcolm Gladwell wrote in an essay last year. "Depression and suicide have soared. A kind of passivity has set in...and the smartphone is the main culprit."

At its best, technology enhances our lives. That's where I think we are headed with AVs. My hope is that they will take from us the tiresome aspects of driving (commuting, primarily) and that, as a society, we'll be smart enough to preserve and celebrate the great parts of our century-old obsession with automobiles and driving that no one wants to lose—going fast, going slow, freedom, self-direction, meandering, tinkering, car shows, road trips, drive-ins, peeling out.

Of course, whether we enjoy the best of both worlds is up to those of us who are inclined, say, to produce or read this far into a heartfelt book called *Never Stop Driving*. Freedom, as they say, isn't free. We tend to get and keep the rights we insist on.

1967 Chevrolet
Camaro RS.
Photo by DW Burnett

With that in mind, I'll leave you with this call to action. It's up to us to preserve and protect our collective automotive past. It's also up to us to create a vision for the future whereby the cars we love to drive are allowed to share the road with cars that drive themselves.

The best way for us to do this is to come together as a community. There are a lot of us, after all. If we speak up, collectively and individually, then a driving future is ensured. We can also share our passion with younger generations and others to keep the love alive. Fix the family car together. Teach your kids and the neighbors' kids how to drive a stick. Take them to car shows and museums.

But most of all, get out there and drive.

And never, ever stop.

—McKeel Hagerty